THE GLORY OF GRACE

TRUTHFORLIFE®

THE BIBLE-TEACHING MINISTRY OF **ALISTAIR BEGG**

The mission of Truth For Life is to teach the Bible with clarity and relevance so that unbelievers will be converted, believers will be established, and local churches will be strengthened.

Daily Program

Each day, Truth For Life distributes the Bible teaching of Alistair Begg across the U.S. and in several locations outside of the U.S. through 1,700 radio outlets. To find a radio station near you, visit **truthforlife.org/stationfinder**.

Free Teaching

The daily program, and Truth For Life's entire teaching archive of over 2,000 Bible-teaching messages, can be accessed for free online and through Truth For Life's full-feature mobile app. Download the free mobile app at **truthforlife.org/app** and listen free online at **truthforlife.org**.

At-Cost Resources

Books and full-length teaching from Alistair Begg on CD, DVD, and USB are available for purchase at cost, with no markup. Visit **truthforlife.org/store**.

Where to Begin?

If you're new to Truth For Life and would like to know where to begin listening and learning, find starting point suggestions at **truthforlife.org/firststep**. For a full list of ways to connect with Truth For Life, visit **truthforlife.org/subscribe**.

Contact Truth For Life

P.O. Box 398000 Cleveland, Ohio 44139
phone 1 (888) 588-7884   **email** letters@truthforlife.org
 /truthforlife @truthforlife truthforlife.org

THE GLORY
OF GRACE

❈

AN INTRODUCTION
TO THE PURITANS
In Their Own Words

Selected and Introduced by
Lewis Allen & Tim Chester

THE BANNER OF TRUTH TRUST

THE BANNER OF TRUTH TRUST

Head Office	*North America Office*
3 Murrayfield Road	PO Box 621
Edinburgh	Carlisle
EH12 6EL	PA 17013
UK	USA

banneroftruth.org

First published 2018
© Lewis Allen & Tim Chester 2018
Reprinted 2019 (special)

*

ISBN

Print: 978 1 84871 834 0
Epub: 978 1 84871 835 7
Kindle: 978 1 84871 836 4

*

Typeset in 12/15 Dante MT
at The Banner of Truth Trust, Edinburgh

Printed in the USA by
Versa Press Inc.,
East Peoria, IL.

CONTENTS

INTRODUCTION
The Puritans

WHO were the Puritans? What did they seek to achieve? What were their successes and failures? Are they of any importance to Christians today? We all know the popular caricature of the Puritans—self-righteous killjoys who were never happier than when they were *un*happy (and everyone else along with them). To be labelled as having 'Puritan' views today means being written off as narrow-minded and oppressed. For many in the church, just as in the world, these apparently gloomy figures are best forgotten.

We firmly believe that, instead of dismissing the Puritan Era as an irrelevant chapter in the 'how they did things then' book of historical curiosities, all Christians need to discover the important story of how these men and women sought to follow Jesus Christ. Their convictions resulted in a brave and joyful faith, and the writing they have left us on the Christian life continues to be a rich resource for our own discipleship. Meeting the Puritans by listening to them has enriched both of us more than we can express. And so we want to introduce you to people who had a deep love for Jesus Christ and a great vision for the Christian life. We all have much to learn.

The term 'Puritan' was used in the late 1500s and 1600s as a label for those who were wholeheartedly committed to the Christian faith as taught in the Bible. They firmly believed the Bible's teaching should shape personal life, the church and the state. The term was often used as a smear-word, as today people might speak of Christians as being 'narrow-minded' or 'over the top'. But those who were called (or who called themselves) 'Puritans' were usually happy to take a bit of slander, if it marked them out as being committed followers of Jesus Christ and his word.

And Puritan ambitions? In 1646 John Geree (a Presbyterian minister in Tewkesbury) wrote a well-known pamphlet *The Character of an Old English Puritane, or Non-conformist*. Geree notes four key Puritan distinctives: (1) a sincere love for God as expressed in the Sunday worship of the local church; (2) an ardent concern for the purity and well-being of the Church of Christ; (3) personal commitment to growing in godliness through the word and prayer; and (4) involvement in society to promote the welfare of the nation and the local community. All of these pursuits were undertaken with the conviction that the Bible was the supreme guide for life and that Christian faith must impact every part of human experience. 'The best Christians should be the best husbands, the best wives, best parents, best children, best masters, best servants, best magistrates.' However much the Puritans were criticized, then and now, there was nothing wrong with their vision for a world transformed to the glory of Christ.

These priorities should seem familiar to those of us who claim to be reformed or evangelical Christians. We are about the same business. We, too, aim to bring all things under the lordship of Christ, to the glory of God. That means that, as we get to know the Puritans, we're not researching some quirky sect from the past, but we're doing a little family history. We're looking at men and women who had dreams just like ours. To know their story is to understand more of God's grace and his ways in lives similar to our own. To get to know the Puritans is to see God's grace in ways which will instruct and encourage us in our own commitment to Christ.

Realizing a Reformation?

The origins of the English Puritan Movement are found nearly a century before Geree's comments in the tail end of the Reformation. The English Reformation began during the reign of Henry VIII and was pursued vigorously during the six-year reign of his son Edward VI (who ruled 1547-53). After his death aged fifteen and the abortive nine day reign of Queen Jane, Edward's staunchly Catholic sister Mary came to the throne. 'Bloody Mary' did all she could to reverse Reformation distinctives, including the harassment and execution of leading churchmen. During the five years of her rule (1553-1558) many church leaders as well as lay people fled to the Continent. In Strasbourg, Frankfurt, Geneva, Zurich and other centres of Protestantism they were eager students of the faith that was coming to be known as 'Reformed' Christianity. When Elizabeth I came to the throne in 1558, they were impatient to return to reform the Church of England according to the word of God.

Elizabeth, while a Protestant, did not welcome the convictions the exiles brought back with them, and so the battle for the soul of the Church of England continued throughout her 45-year reign. More concerned with political rule than church reform, Elizabeth did not support of the Puritan cause. She wanted her church to be Protestant, but, to the horror of the Puritans, she also wanted to retain many of the trappings of its Catholic past. This approach—known as 'the Elizabethan Settlement'—was enforced in the (third) Act of Uniformity (1559). The Puritans pressed for further reform in keeping with the practices of continental Protestantism. Although their movement was strengthened by a stellar cast of preachers and civic leaders, Puritan ambitions for the church were frustrated at every turn as Elizabeth's reign progressed. In 1593 failure to conform to the Church of England's doctrine or to absent oneself from the worship of the local parish church were punishable by loss of goods and even exile. The Puritans had effectively lost the battle for the national church by the end of the 1500s.

The new century ushered in no new hope for the Puritans. In 1603 James I (James VI of Scotland) came to the throne and made it clear he intended to leave things pretty much as they were. Some Puritan ministers conformed as little as possible and used the parish church as a centre for preaching and pastoral work. The Archbishop of Canterbury, John Whitgift, although enforcing the 'Elizabethan Settlement', undertook reforms of the church and made common cause with the Puritans in promoting Calvinist orthodoxy. Others, however, left the Church of England and became persecuted 'Separatists'—members of independent congregations. In 1625 Charles I became King and in 1633 William Laud became Archbishop of Canterbury. Not only did both like Catholic ceremonies, both were Arminians, and so were fiercely opposed to the Calvinism of the Puritans. How much longer were the Puritans ready to wait? Many saw a new life overseas as their only option if they were to worship God according to the Bible and their consciences. The Pilgrim Fathers who left England for the new world of America in 1620 were Puritans escaping religious persecution. In 1630 a large number left England for Massachusetts to join the project of creating a 'New England'—a pure church and state governed according to Puritan principles. Those who remained found their convictions sorely tested, and their non-compliance with the Church of England punishable by fines and confiscation of property.

Servants of a Nation

The English Civil War led to defeat for the monarchy and the creation of the 'Commonwealth' (1649–1660) under the leadership of Oliver Cromwell. Now at last the Puritans had an unparalleled opportunity to implement their agenda. Whatever the misgivings held by Puritans about the execution of Charles I—and there were many—the godly were united in their belief that the Lord had given them an open door to bring reformation according to the word of God to church and people. The Puritans had been opposed, harassed and humiliated. Now they believed that their time had come.

This period saw one of Puritanism's greatest strengths coming to the fore, as a dynamic movement of education and learning. In 1643, while the civil war still raged, Parliament convened the Westminster Assembly to provide guidelines for the reform of the church and give expression to Puritan faith. It brought together some of the finest minds in the land who wrestled with how to formulate the faith of the Bible. Over 100 English Puritan leaders, plus representatives from Scotland, met in sessions over the next ten years. The resulting Westminster Confession of Faith and the Longer and Shorter Westminster Catechisms are regarded as the primary statement of Puritan and Reformed theology in the English-speaking world. The Church of Scotland adopted the Confession in the following year, 1647, and it remains the confession of Presbyterian churches. Adapted forms were adopted by American Congregationalists (The Cambridge Platform) in 1648, English Congregationalists (The Savoy Declaration) in 1658 and Baptists in 1677 (the London Baptist Confession, as a reissuing of a confession published in 1644).

With such declarations of the faith the Puritans might have thought that their movement would be a powerful force. The country, however, was broken by the civil war and in no mood for religious innovations. The war had been a drawn-out affair, devastating large parts of the country and splitting communities (a greater proportion of population of the British Isles lost their lives in the civil war than did in the First World War). The war was rightly seen as a conflict due in large part to religious grievances. Wounds would take decades to heal. Try as they did—and they tried valiantly—the Puritans had a hard task bringing religious and social reformation to a culture which was suspicious of those they saw as responsible for the conflict. New laws were put into place against many social vices (by any modern estimate, not always wisely or well), but it was obvious that the English did not want Puritan piety. The leading Puritan minister Richard Baxter defended the Commonwealth ideal as less a failed experiment, but rather as a project which wasn't allowed sufficient time. With amazing optimism he conjectured that, given twenty five years, it would have transformed England into being a true land of saints. Others were far less convinced.

Discipleship on the Margins

By 1660 the freedoms of Cromwell's rule opened up divisions among the Puritans, witnessing splits of Presbyterians, Congregationalist and Baptists, as well as between Quakers and other groups. When Cromwell died there was no one suitable to replace him and the nation returned to the monarchy under Charles II. By this point Puritanism was no longer a political force. With the restoration of the monarchy there was a new regime. The new leadership of the Church of England was determined to extinguish even the memory of Puritanism. Laws were immediately passed requiring the attendance of all at their local parish church with harsh penalties for failure to comply. Worse was to come. In 1662 over 2,000 ministers in the Church of England were forced to leave in what was known as 'the Great Ejection'. The

Church of England lost some of its finest servants and from that point onwards the distinctives of Puritanism would be more often found outside that Church. The failure of the Puritan vision and the triumphs of its opponents by 1662 were colossal. In twenty years all to which the Commonwealth had aspired was in ruins.

The 1660s and 1670s saw Puritan believers coming to terms with their struggles. Meetings for worship and preaching were often held in secluded places with men posted to keep a lookout for the king's soldiers. Gospel preachers were imprisoned or fined. Some leaders and their people grew disillusioned and opted for an easier existence. For many others, though, the testing of their faith brought out a Spirit-given courage to live for their Master, remembering that he suffered in order to set for them an example.

John Bunyan wrote his *Pilgrim's Progress* during his imprisonment of 1661–72. His main theme—the Christian life as pilgrimage and unceasing warfare—met a receptive audience. In the book the heaven for which Christian longs has not been built on earth, nor can it be. It is the prize for those who are faithful unto death. Christian and his fellow-travellers are despised and vulnerable as they journey to the Celestial City. Puritanism had learned much from its broken dreams and had its eye set more firmly than ever on heaven.

Relief was found in the Revolution of 1688, when James II's three year reign (following his brother Charles II) was swept away by William of Orange. Promises of liberty were made to those with Puritan convictions, but their freedom to worship still came at a price, which many felt was insulting and unfair. For all of their hopes for freedom and influence in society, the Puritan successors found themselves very much the second-class citizens they were a quarter of a century before. Their day had not come. Two Puritans who lived through this later period require special mention. John Owen (1616–1683) is called 'the Prince of the Puritans'. He was a chaplain in the army of Oliver Cromwell and vice-chancellor of Oxford University, but most of his life he served as a church minister. His written works run to 24 volumes and represent the best resource for theology in the English language. On several important subjects such as the Holy Spirit, mortification of sin and apostasy, he is unexcelled. Richard Baxter (1615–1691) was a devoted pastor whose ministry at Kidderminster in Worcestershire left an indelible mark on the town. A prolific writer, his work *The Christian Directory* consists of a detailed application of the gospel to every aspect of life. This is probably the most comprehensive exposition of its kind ever written.

The theology, spirituality and pastoral insight of Puritanism continue to be a source of instruction and inspiration to many evangelicals. Here are four reasons why the Puritans remain important today:

1. The Puritans Learned to Discover Grace in Suffering

For all of their zeal, the Puritans never saw anything like the nationwide gospel-impact for which they longed. Their ministries and efforts were often opposed. And so they were compelled to go back to their Lord to find strength for their journey. It's no wonder that some of the most enduring Puritan works concern discipleship in suffering.

2. The Puritans Were Committed to Learning and Education

They believed that the Bible was a book for all to understand and live out. Their love for God's word set British Christianity in a direction which is still bearing fruit in much of today's evangelicalism. Puritan convictions about the place of the Bible in personal and public life have left an enduring legacy. These men and woman are a lasting example to us that, if we want to be full of God's Spirit, we must be full of his word.

3. The Puritans Longed to See the Power of Gospel Transformation

Why all the books, the pamphlets, the sermons, the small group teaching? The Puritans didn't prize learning for its own sake, but as God's appointed means for effecting real change in a believer's life. The Puritans believed that, when the Bible's truth is understood in the power of the Spirit, the Spirit brings growth in Christ and practical transformation. Their best writing serves as a guide to the gospel in the everyday life.

4. The Puritans Wanted to Know God, Above All

These men and women were not the eggheads or the kill-joys of popular caricature. They were Christians who wanted to walk with God and who wanted others to share in their discovery of Jesus Christ. Puritan ministers unashamedly preached for conversion, and church members equally longed to share their faith with friends and neighbours. Puritan encouraged a rich and living personal devotion to God. The Puritans wanted to see the world conquered by the gospel of grace, but they wanted their own hearts conquered first. Through their prayer, learning and gospel-living, they set a challenging example to us.

Our aim is for you to hear the Puritans in their own words. The chapters in this book have been selected for their pastoral benefit. They're presented in the approximate order in which they were first written. You'll meet great men and a great woman. You'll listen to their insights on how to know God and live a life of fruitful discipleship. Some of the chapters we've chosen contain discussions of theology which will make you think hard. Please do. The Puritans wanted a *deep* devotion to God in Christ and therefore they weren't afraid to think deeply about what the Bible teaches. Every chapter has been selected to help us as Christians. The Puritans always wanted their writing to lead them to moment-by-moment worship with full hearts ready to engage both fellow believers and a needy world with the gospel.

The main problem modern readers meet when encountering the Puritans is that the style in which they wrote is no longer familiar to us. So we have gently edited their work to make it more digestible. We've reshaped sentences to aid clarity. We've replaced archaic words with contemporary equivalents. And we've added headings to signpost the argument. Our prayer is that meeting these authors will be the start of a rewarding friendship with them.

Further Reading

- Joel R. Beeke and Mark Jones, *A Puritan Theology: Doctrine for Life* (Grand Rapids: Reformation Heritage Books, 2012).

- Joel R. Beeke and Randall Pederson, *Meet the Puritans*, (Grand Rapids: Reformation Heritage Books, 2006).

- John Coffey and Paul C. H. Lim (eds.), *The Cambridge Companion to Puritanism* (Cambridge: CUP, 2008).

- Kelly M. Kapic and Randall C. Gleason, *The Devoted Life: An Invitation to the Puritan Classics*, (Downers Grove, IL: InterVarsity Press, 2004).

- Peter Lewis, *The Genius of Puritanism,* (Haywards Heath: Carey Publications, 1979).

- J. I. Packer, *Among God's Giants: The Puritan Vision of the Christian Life* (Eastbourne: Kingsway, 1991). (Originally published in the USA by Crossway under the title *A Quest for Godliness*).

- Leland Ryken, *Worldly Saints: The Puritans As They Really Were*, Zondervan, 1986.

- Many Puritan works are also available online. The best place to start is digitalpuritan.net which gathers together links from across the internet.

RICHARD SIBBES
on Assurance

I followed sermons, pursuing the means, and was constant in duties and doing, looking for Heaven that way. And then I was so precise for outward formalities, that I censured all to be reprobates ... But yet I was distracted in my mind, wounded in conscience, and wept often and bitterly, and prayed earnestly, but yet had no comfort, till I heard that sweet saint ... Doctor Sibbes, by whose means and ministry I was brought to peace and joy in my spirit. His sweet soul-melting Gospel-sermons won my heart and refreshed me much, for by him I saw and had much of God and was confident in Christ.

S O wrote Humphrey Mills, describing his experience of hearing the preaching of Richard Sibbes (1577–1635).

Sibbes was born in Suffolk, the son of a wheelwright, and converted as a student at Cambridge. In 1610 he became lecturer at Holy Trinity in Cambridge, but was fired five years later because of his Puritan convictions. By now Sibbes was well known for his heart-warming preaching, so in 1617 he was appointed the preacher at Gray's Inn, one of the most influential pulpits in London. In 1626 he became the Master of St Catharine's Hall, Cambridge, and in 1633 he returned to

Holy Trinity, this time by crown appointment. Sibbes continued his ministry in both Cambridge and London until his death in 1635, aged 58.

The Bruised Reed and Smoking Flax (1631) was written, Sibbes says, 'for the good of weaker Christians.' Sibbes uses the metaphor of *bruising* to describes the process by which God enlightens sinners. God must reveal to us our need for salvation before we turn to him for mercy. He must wound before he can heal. But Sibbes' focus is the healing work of God. His aim was to lead people to a strong sense of assurance by showing them the 'free offer of grace'. The tone is set in the opening paragraphs:

> What a support to our faith is this, that God the father, the party offended by our sins, is so well pleased with the work of redemption! And what a comfort is this, that seeing God's love rests on Christ, as well pleased in him, we may gather that he is as well pleased with us, if we be in Christ!

Things To Look Out For

There was a polemic edge to Sibbes' writing. He was challenging the tendency toward destructive self-absorption that came from examining one's own behaviours for signs of grace to gain assurance of salvation. Some early Puritans urged troubled Christians to more duty. Sibbes urges them to behold Christ. Sibbes also urges pastors to be gentle with their congregations, not laying expectations on them that they are not able to bear.

One of the big questions Puritans wrestled with was how someone could know whether they were one of Christ's elect people. Some put the emphasis on the fruit of conversion in a person's life. The danger with this, though, is that it could lead to an unhealthy introspection. In contrast Sibbes invites us to look away from ourselves to Christ. Our assurance is found in Christ and his finished work, not in ourselves.

In the final part of the book, Sibbes interprets the reference to Christ sending 'forth judgment under victory' as his work of sanctification in the heart of a believer. Many Puritans became focused on the rule of Christ in the world, either through the English Civil War or by emigrating to America to create a new society. But Sibbes was among those who focused on the rule of Christ in the soul.

Sibbes also emphasized the impact of knowing Christ upon our affections (our desires or motives). We do not change simply by deciding to do better. What the will decides to do matters, but the will is governed by our affections. So change takes place as our affections are won for Christ. We are wooed by Christ. So Sibbes believed the law may be used to confront sin. But our central message must be God's love in Christ. If we find ourselves struggling to obey Christ, the solution is 'to warm ourselves at this fire of his love and mercy in giving himself for us.'

❋

The Bruised Reed

> A bruised reed he will not break,
> and a smouldering wick he will not quench,
> until he brings justice to victory.
>
> *Matthew 12:20*

Chapters 1–3[1]

The Reed and the Bruising

The prophet Isaiah being lifted up, and carried with the wing of prophetic spirit, passes over all the time between him and

---

[1] *The Works of Richard Sibbes,* Vol. 1 (Edinburgh: Banner of Truth, 1973, repr. 2001), pp. 42-46.

the appearing of Jesus Christ in the flesh, and sees with the eye of prophecy, and with the eye of faith, Christ as present, and presents him, in the name of God, to the spiritual eye of others, in these words: 'Behold my servant whom I have chosen' (cf. Isa. 43:10). In Matthew 12, St Matthew claims this is fulfilled now in Christ (Matt. 12:18). Here is propounded, first, the calling of Christ to his office, and secondly, the execution of it.

1. The Calling of Christ to His Office

God describes him here as his righteous servant. Christ was God's servant in the greatest piece of service that ever was—a chosen and a choice servant. He did and suffered all by commission from the Father. Here we may see the sweet love of God to us, that counts the work of our salvation by Christ his greatest service; and that he will put his only beloved Son to that service.

He might well begin 'Behold' to raise up our thoughts to the highest pitch of attention and admiration. In time of temptation, misgiving consciences look so much on the present trouble they are in, that they need be roused up to behold him in whom they may find rest for their distressed souls. In temptations it is safest to behold nothing but Christ, the true Bronze Serpent (John 3:14-15), the true Lamb of God that takes away the sins of the world (John 1:29). This saving object has a special influence of comfort on the soul, especially if we look not only on Christ, but upon the Father's authority and love in him. For in all that Christ did and suffered as Mediator, we must see God in him reconciling the world to himself (2 Cor. 5:19).

What a support to our faith is this, that God the Father, the party offended by our sins, is so well pleased with the work of redemption! And what a comfort is this, that seeing God's love rests on Christ, as well-pleased in him, we may gather that he is as well pleased with us, if we be in Christ! For his love rests in the whole Christ, in Christ mystical [the Church, the spiritual body of Christ], as well as Christ natural, because he loves him and us with one love. Let us, therefore, embrace Christ, and in him God's love, and build our faith safely on such a Saviour, that is furnished with so high a commission.

See here, for our comfort, a sweet agreement of all three persons: the Father gives a commission to Christ; the Spirit furnishes and sanctifies it; Christ himself executes the office of a Mediator. Our redemption is founded upon the joint agreement of all three persons of the Trinity.

2. The Execution of His Calling

The execution of this his calling is set down here to be modest, without making a noise, or raising dust by any pompous coming, as princes usually do. 'His voice shall not be heard.' His voice indeed was heard, but what voice? 'Come unto me, all you that are weary and heavy laden' (Matt. 11:28 KJV). He cried, but how? 'Ho, every one that thirsts, come' (Isa. 55:1 KJV). And as his coming was modest, so it was mild, which is set down in these words: *the bruised reed shall he not break*. Here we may observe these three things:

1. First, the condition of those that Christ had to deal with: They were bruised reeds and smoking flax.

2. Second, Christ's conduct towards them. He did not break the bruised reed, nor quenched the smoking flax. Here more is meant than is said. For he will not only not break the bruised reed, nor quench the smoking flax, but he will cherish them.

3. Third, the constancy and progress of this his tender care, 'until judgment come to victory'—that is, until the sanctified frame of grace begun in their hearts be

brought to that perfection, so that it prevails over all opposite corruption.

The Condition of Christ's People

For the *first*, the condition of men whom he was to deal with is that they were bruised reeds and smoking flax. They were not trees, but reeds, and not whole, but bruised reeds. The church is compared to weak things: to a dove among the fowls; to a vine among the plants; to sheep among the beasts; to a woman, who is the weaker vessel. And here God's children are compared to bruised reeds and smoking flax.

They are bruised reeds before their conversion, and often afterwards. Before conversion all (except such as being brought up in the church, to whom God delighted to show himself gracious from their childhood) are bruised. Yet they are bruised in different degrees, as God sees appropriate. As their difference is in regard of temper, parts, manner of life and so on, so in God's plan of employment for the time to come. For usually he empties people of themselves, and makes them nothing, before he will use them in any great services.

This bruised reed is a man that for the most part is in some misery, as those were that came to Christ for help, and by this misery is brought to see sin which causes it. For whatever pretences sin makes, bruising or breaking exposes. So he is aware of sin and misery, even bruising. And, seeing no help in himself, is carried with restless desire to be supplied by another. He has some hope, a little of which raises him out of himself to Christ, though he dares not claim any present experience of mercy.

This spark of hope, being opposed by doubtings and fears arising from corruption, makes him like smoking flax. So that both these together, a bruised reed and smoking flax, make up the state of a poor distressed man. Such a one our Saviour

Christ terms 'poor in spirit' (Matt. 5:3), who sees a want, and sees himself indebted to divine justice, and sees no means of supply from himself or from any other creature, and therefore mourns. Upon some hope of mercy from the promise and from examples of those that have obtained mercy, he is stirred up to hunger and thirst after it.

1. We Need Bruising Before Conversion

This bruising is required *before conversion* so that the Spirit may make way for himself in the heart by levelling all proud, high thoughts, and that we may understand ourselves to be what indeed we are by nature. We love to wander from ourselves and to be strangers at home, till God bruises us by one cross or other, and then we think to ourselves, and come home to ourselves with the prodigal (Luke 15:17).

A marvellous hard thing it is to bring a dull and a shifting heart to cry with feeling for mercy. Our hearts, like malefactors, until they are beaten from all waywardness, never cry for the mercy of the Judge.

Again, this bruising makes us set a high price upon Christ. The gospel is good news indeed then. Then the fig-leaves of morality will do us no good. And this bruising makes us more thankful. From thankfulness comes more fruit in our lives. For what makes many so cold and barren, but that bruising for sin never endeared God's grace unto them?

Likewise, this dealing of God establishes us the more in his ways, having had knocks and bruisings in our own ways. This is often the cause of relapses and apostasies, because men never smarted for sin at the beginning. They were not long enough under the lash of the law. Hence this inferior work of the Spirit [inferior because it is not the Spirit's ultimate goal] in bringing down high thoughts (2 Cor. 10:5) is necessary before conversion. And, for the most part, the Holy

Spirit, to further the work of conviction, joins some affliction, which, sanctified, has a healing and purging power.

2. We Need Bruising After Conversion

We also need bruising after conversion, so that reeds may know themselves to be reeds, and not oaks. Even reeds need bruising because of the remainder of pride in our nature, and to let us see that we live by mercy.

It also means weaker Christians are not too much discouraged when they see stronger Christians shaken and bruised. Thus Peter was bruised when he wept bitterly (Matt. 26:75). This reed, till he met with this bruise, had more wind in him than pith. 'Though all forsake thee,' he claimed, 'I will not.' (cf. Matt. 26:35). The people of God cannot be without these examples. The heroic deeds of those great worthies do not comfort the church so much as their falls and bruises do. Thus David was bruised (Psa. 32:3-5), until he came to a free confession, without guile of spirit. Indeed, his sorrows rose in his feelings like the exquisite pain of breaking of bones (Psa. 51:8). Thus Hezekiah complains that God had broken his bones as a lion (Isa. 38:13). Thus the chosen vessel St Paul needed the messenger of Satan to buffet him, lest he should be lifted up above measure (2 Cor. 12:7).

Hence we learn that we must not pass too harsh a judgment upon ourselves or others when God exercises us with bruising upon bruising. There must be a conformity to our head, Christ, who was bruised for us (Isa. 53:5), that we may know how much we are bound unto him. Profane spirits, ignorant of God's ways in bringing his children to heaven, censure broken-hearted Christians as desperate persons, when in fact God is doing a gracious and good work with them. It is no easy matter to bring a man from nature to grace, and from grace to glory, so unyielding and untractable are our hearts.

The Conduct of Christ

The second point is that Christ will not 'break the bruised reed.' Physicians, though they put their patients to much pain, yet they will not destroy nature, but raise it up by degrees. Surgeons will lance and cut, but not dismember. A mother that has a sick and difficult child will not therefore cast it away. And shall there be more mercy in the stream than in the spring? Shall we think there is more mercy in ourselves than in God, who plants the affection of mercy in us?

But for a further declaration of Christ's mercy to all bruised reeds, consider the comforting relationships he has taken upon himself of husband, shepherd, brother, and so on, which he will fulfil to the very end. For shall others by his grace fulfil what he calls them to, and not he that, out of his love, has taken upon him these relationships, so thoroughly founded upon his Father's assignment and his own voluntary undertaking? Consider his borrowed names from the mildest creatures: as lamb, hen, and so on, to show his tender care. Consider his very name 'Jesus', a Saviour, given him by God himself. Consider the office that corresponds to this name, which is that he should 'bind up the broken-hearted' (Isa. 61:1). At his baptism the Holy Spirit sat on him in the shape of a dove to show that he should be a dove-like, gentle Mediator. See the gracious manner of executing his offices.

Prophet

As a *prophet*, he came with blessing in his mouth: 'Blessed are the poor in spirit' (Matt. 5:3). And he invited those to come to him whose hearts suggested most exceptions against themselves: 'Come unto me, all you that are weary and heavy-laden' (Matt. 11:28 KJV). How did his heart yearn when he saw the people as 'sheep without a shepherd' (Matt. 9:36)! He never turned any back that came to him, though some went away of their own accord.

Priest

He came to die as a *priest* for his enemies. In the days of his flesh he dictated a form of prayer to his disciples, and put petitions to God into their mouths, and his Spirit to intercede in their hearts. And now he makes intercession in heaven for weak Christians, standing between God's anger and them. He shed tears for those that shed his blood.

King

So he is a meek *King*. He will admit mourners into his presence, a king of poor and afflicted persons. As he has beams of majesty, so he has a heart of mercy and compassion. He is 'a prince of peace' (Isa. 9:6). Why was he tempted, but that he might succour those that are tempted (Heb. 2:18)?

What mercy may we not expect from so gracious a mediator (1 Tim. 2:5), that took our nature upon him that he might be gracious? He is a physician good at all diseases, especially at binding up a broken heart. He died that he might heal our souls with a plaster of his own blood, and by that death save us, the death we procured for ourselves by our own sins. And has he not the same heart in heaven? 'Saul, Saul, why are you persecuting me?' cried the Head [of the church] in heaven (Acts 9:4), when the foot was trodden on, on earth. His advancement [to glory] has not made him forget his own flesh. Though it has freed him from suffering, it has not freed him from compassion towards us. The Lion of the tribe of Judah will only tear in pieces those that will not have him rule over them (Luke 19:14). He will not show his strength against those that prostrate themselves before him.

What Should We Learn From This?

First, 'to come boldly to the throne of grace' in all our grievances (cf. Heb. 4:16). Shall our sins discourage us, when he appears there only for sinners? Are you bruised? Be of good comfort, he calls you. Do not conceal your wounds; open all before him. Do not keep Satan's counsel. Go to Christ, though trembling as the poor woman. If we can but 'touch the hem of his garment' (cf. Matt. 9:20), we shall be healed and have a gracious answer. Go boldly to God in your flesh. For this reason—that we might go boldly to him—he is flesh of our flesh, and bone of our bone. Never fear to go to God, since we have such a Mediator with him who is not only our friend, but our brother and husband. Well might the angels proclaim from heaven, 'Behold, we bring you tidings of joy' (cf. Luke 2:10). Well might the Apostle stir us up to 'rejoice in the Lord again and again' (cf. Phil. 4:4) – he was well advised on what grounds he did it. Peace and joy are two main fruits of Christ's kingdom. Let the world be as it will, if we cannot rejoice in the world, yet we may rejoice in the Lord. His presence makes any condition comfortable. 'Be not afraid,' he said to his disciples, when they were afraid as if they had seen a ghost, 'it is I' (cf. Matt. 14:27), as if there were no cause of fear where he is present.

Second, let this stay us when we feel ourselves bruised. Christ's plan is first to wound, then to heal. No sound, whole soul shall ever enter into heaven. Think in temptation, Christ was tempted for me. According to my trials will be my graces and comforts. If Christ be so merciful as not to break me, I will not break myself by despair, nor yield myself over to the roaring lion Satan, to break me in pieces.

Third, see the contrasting dispositions of Christ, and Satan and his instruments. Satan sets upon us when we are weakest, as Simeon and Levi upon the Shechemites, 'when they were sore' (Gen. 34:25). But Christ will make up in us all the breaches sin and Satan have made. He 'binds up the broken-hearted' (cf. Isa. 61:1). As a mother tends most to the most diseased and weakest child, so Christ most mercifully inclines to the weakest, and likewise puts an instinct into the weakest things to rely upon something stronger than themselves for support. The vine stays itself upon the elm and the weakest creatures often have the strongest shelters. The consciousness of the church's weakness makes her willing to lean on her beloved, and to hide herself under his wing.

Chapters 18–19[2]

The Nature of Christ's Judgment and Victory

We come to the constant progress of Christ's gracious power, until he sets up such an absolute government in us as shall prevail over all corruptions. It is said here he will cherish his beginnings of grace in us until he brings judgment to victory. By judgment here is meant the kingdom of grace in us, that government in which Christ sets up a throne in our hearts. Governors among the Jews were first called judges, then kings. Therefore this inward rule is called 'judgment'. This inward rule or judgment also agrees with the outward judgment of God's word, which the psalmist often calls 'judgment' (Psa. 72:1-2 KJV) because it agrees with God's judgment. Men may read their doom in God's word. What it judges of them, God judges of them. By this judgment set up in us, good is discerned, allowed, and performed; sin is judged, condemned, and executed. Our spirit, being under the Spirit of Christ, is governed by him, and so far as it is governed by Christ, we are governed graciously.

Christ and we are of one judgment, and of one will. He has his will in us; and his judgments are so invested in us, that they are turned into our judgment, and we carry his law in our hearts, written by his Spirit (Jer. 31:33). The law in the inner man and the law written down become a mirror of each other.

[2] *The Works of Richard Sibbes*, Vol. 1 (Edinburgh: Banner of Truth, 1973, repr. 2001), pp. 77-80.

The meaning of this then is that the gracious frame of holiness set up in our hearts by the Spirit of Christ shall go forward until all contrary power be brought under control. The spirit of judgment will be a spirit of burning (Isa. 4:4), to consume whatever opposes corruption, like rust eats into the soul. If God's builders fall into errors, and build with stubble upon a good foundation, God's Spirit, as a spiritual 'fire will reveal this in time' (cf. 1 Cor. 3:13), and destroy it. They shall, by a spirit of judgment, condemn their own errors and courses [of action]. The whole work of grace in us is set out under the name of judgment, and sometimes wisdom, because judgment is the chief and leading part in grace. Therefore that gracious work of repentance is called a change of the mind, and also an act of wisdom. In the learned languages, the words that express wisdom imply the general relish and savour of the whole soul, and rather more the judgment of taste than of sight, or any other sense, because taste is the most necessary sense, and requires the nearest application of the object compared with the other senses. So in spiritual life, it is most necessary that the Spirit should alter the taste of the soul, so as that it might savour the things of the Spirit so deeply, that all other things should be out of relish.

Just as it is true of every particular Christian that Christ's judgment in him shall be victorious, so likewise of the whole body of Christians—the church. The government of Christ, and his truth, by which he rules as by a sceptre, shall at length be victorious—in spite of Satan, antichrist, and all enemies. Christ riding on his white horse has a bow, and goes forth conquering (Rev. 6:2; 19:11) in the ministry that he may overcome, either to [produce] conversion or confusion. Yet I take judgment to mean Christ's kingdom and government *within us* principally: 1. Because God especially requires the subjection of the soul and conscience as his proper throne. 2. Because if judgment should prevail in all others about us and not in our own hearts, it would not yield comfort to us. This therefore is the first thing that we desire when we pray, 'Your kingdom come', that Christ would come and rule in our hearts. The kingdom of Christ in his ordinances [within the church] serves but to bring Christ home to his own place, our hearts.

The words being thus explained, that judgment here includes the government of both mind, will, and affections, there are various conclusions that naturally spring from them.

Christ Will Govern Those Who Enjoy the Comfort of His Mildness

The first conclusion from the connection of this part of the verse with the first part is that Christ is mild and so he will set up his government in those over whom he is gentle and tender. He so pardons that he will be obeyed as a king; he so takes us to be his spouse that he will be obeyed as a husband. The same Spirit that convinces us of the necessity of his righteousness to cover us, convinces us also of the necessity of his government to rule us. His love to us moves him to frame us to be like himself, and our love to him stirs us up to become such as he may take delight in. Our faith or hope never exceed our desire to be purged as he is pure. He makes us subordinate governors, yes, kings under himself, giving us grace not only to oppose, but to subdue in some measure our base affections. It is one of the main fruits of Christ's exaltation that he may turn every one of us from our wickedness (Acts 3:26). 'For to this end Christ died and lived again, that he might be Lord both of the dead and of the living' (Rom. 14:9). God has bound himself by an oath that he would grant us this, that 'without fear we might serve him in holiness and righteousness in his sight' (cf. Luke 1:74-75), not only in the sight of the world.

This may serve for a trial [or test] to discern who may lay just claim to Christ's mercy:

- those that will take his yoke, and count it a greater happiness to be under his government, than to enjoy any liberty of the flesh;

- those that will take whole Christ, and not single out of him what may stand with their present contentment;

- those that will not divide 'Lord' from 'Jesus', and so make a Christ of their own.

No-one ever truly desires *pardoning* mercy, without also desiring *healing* mercy. David prays for a new spirit as well as for sense of pardoning mercy (Psa. 51:10).

This shows that those who make Christ to be only righteousness to us, and not sanctification (except by imputation), are misled. It is a great part of our happiness to be under such a Lord, who was not only born for us and given to us, but 'has the government likewise upon his shoulders,' (cf. Isa. 9:6-7) We are happy because he is our Sanctifier as well as our Saviour. He is our Saviour just as much for the power of sin by the effectual power of his Spirit as from the guilt of sin by the merit of his death. Remember that the first and chief ground of our comfort is that Christ as a priest offered himself as a sacrifice to his Father for us. The guilty soul flies first to Christ crucified, made a curse for us. It as a result of this that Christ has the right to govern us, and so it is that he gives us his Spirit as our guide to lead us home.

In the course of our life, after we are in a state of grace, and be overtaken with any sin, we must remember to have recourse first to Christ's mercy to pardon us, and then to the promise of his Spirit to govern us.

And when we feel ourselves cold in affection and duty, the best way to warm ourselves is at this fire of his love and mercy in giving himself for us.

Again, remember this, that Christ, as he rules us, does so by a spirit of love from a sense of his love, so that his commandments are easy to us. He leads us by his free Spirit, a Spirit of liberty. His subjects are voluntary recruits. The constraint that he lays on his subjects is that of love. He draws us with the cords of love sweetly. Yet remember also that he draws us strongly by a Spirit of power. For it is not sufficient that we have motives and encouragements to love and obey Christ from that love of his by which he gave himself for us to justify us. But Christ's Spirit must also subdue our hearts, and sanctify them to love him, without which all motives would be ineffective. Our disposition must be changed; we must be new creatures. They seek for heaven in hell who seek for spiritual love in an unchanged heart. When a child obeys his father, it is so because of reasons persuading him, and a child-like nature gives strength to these reasons. It is natural for a child of God to love Christ so far as he is renewed, not only from the inducement of reason to do so, but also from an inward principle and work of grace. It is by this work of grace that those reasons have their chief force. For we are made partakers of the divine nature, and then we are easily induced and led by Christ's Spirit to spiritual duties.

Further Reading

- Richard Sibbes, *The Bruised Reed* (Edinburgh: Banner of Truth, 2011).

- Richard Sibbes, *The Tender Heart* (Edinburgh: Banner of Truth, 2011).

- *The Works of Richard Sibbes,* 7 vols. (Edinburgh: Banner of Truth, 2001).

- R. N. Frost, *Richard Sibbes: God's Spreading Goodness,* (Chippenham: Cor Deo Press, 2012).

2

THOMAS GOODWIN
on the Holy Spirit

D ESPITE being told as a fourteen-year-old that he was
too short to become a person of spiritual stature,
Thomas Goodwin (1600–1680) in fact went on to be a giant in
the cause of Christ. Goodwin was an outstanding minister of
the gospel who exercised national influence as preacher, theologian and leader. His proved to be a long and full life—few
people made it to seventy-nine in the seventeenth century as
Goodwin did.

Goodwin was born in Norfolk in 1600. Sent off to Cambridge University as a twelve-year-old, he was shaped by the
ministries of Richard Sibbes at Trinity Church, and his suc-
cessor, John Preston. Goodwin became a lecturer at nineteen
and the following year came to a saving knowledge of Christ.
But it was not until eight years later that this knowledge
developed into a full assurance of salvation.

Called to pastor Preston's church after him, Goodwin's
preaching soon filled the pews with eager hearers. One of his
friends, John Cotton, persuaded Goodwin that independency
(or congregationalism, as we would call it today) was the biblical position on church order. Goodwin resigned his post in
1634 and moved to London where he married and ministered
for five years. He then left to pastor a congregation in the
more tolerant environment of Holland.

Thomas Goodwin's return to England coincided with the opening of the Westminster Assembly, the body convened by Parliament to draw up new statements of faith and order for the national church. Goodwin was by far the most active speaker in the debates and he left the clear stamp of his convictions on several theological matters on what became the Westminster Confession. To the frustration of the Presbyterian majority, Goodwin and the four other Independents argued for their model of church government. The Independents' were overruled and Goodwin later joined John Owen in framing the Savoy Declaration in 1658, the major confession for independent churches for centuries to come.

After a hectic pace of preaching, debating and writing in London in the 1640s, Goodwin was President of Magdalen Hall in Oxford for ten years, until Charles II forced his resignation in 1660. The next twenty years saw Goodwin in London, pastoring, writing and working, while coping with various levels of harassment. It was a period when non-conformists faced restrictions on their ministries, including fines and imprisonment. The majority of Goodwin's library was burned in the Great Fire of 1666, though miraculously his theological books survived.

Goodwin's last days were full of grace. He preached right until his death. Among his last words he said, 'I am going to the three Persons, with whom I have had communion: they have taken me; I did not take them. I think I cannot love Christ better than I do; I am swallowed up in God.' This tone of assurance and delight in the Saviour's love, which so characterized his ministry, was on his lips and in his heart at the end.

Things to Look Out For

Our excerpt is a sermon which Goodwin preached on Ephesians 1:14, part of a series of thirty-six sermons on Ephesians 1. Goodwin is known for writings on the Holy Spirit, and in this sermon he explores the gift of the Holy Spirit in the believer's life. The Spirit is a deposit, guaranteeing our salvation. He is also God's seal, empowering us to enjoy a deep, personal assurance that we belong to Christ.

Goodwin's emphasis is slightly different from that of Richard Sibbes (though some people exaggerate those differences). Sibbes exhorts us to look in faith to the finished work of Christ and the promise of God if we want assurance that we are saved. Goodwin agrees, but he puts more emphasis on the believer's experience of the Holy Spirit. While God's promises are the ultimate ground of our assurance, believers can expect to know the Spirit working to make the certainties of God's love powerfully real in our lives. Remember that for many years Goodwin struggled to know this assurance for himself. Once he received it, his life and ministry were transformed.

※

An Exposition of the First Chapter of the Epistle to the Ephesians

From Sermon XVII: Who is the Earnest of our Inheritance until the Redemption of the Purchased Possession, unto the Praise of his Glory[1]

> The promised Holy Spirit,
> who is the guarantee of our inheritance
> until we acquire possession of it,
> to the praise of his glory.
> *Ephesians 1:13-14*

When the apostle Paul speaks of heaven as a thing promised, he mentions the seal of the Spirit: You 'were sealed with the

[1] *The Works of Thomas Goodwin*, Vol. 1 (Edinburgh: James Nichol, 1861), pp. 253-267.

promised Holy Spirit' (Eph. 1:13). When he speaks of heaven as a thing to be possessed and enjoyed, he uses the metaphor of a deposit, which gives a kind of possession beforehand.

A Foretaste of Heaven in the Person of the Spirit

It is true that he mentions the Spirit being a deposit in a special manner in respect of also assuring us of salvation, for the scope of a deposit is to assure as well as to seal. But it is not to be limited only to the work of assurance (though he has that especially in his eye), but it is spoken in a large and more general sense. Paul speaks of the Spirit in respect of all he is to us and all the work he performs in us. In a word, he is not only a deposit in respect of working an assurance in our hearts, but he is a deposit in his Person given to us in his graces wrought in us. ...

You think, if you get grace in your hearts, there is a deposit of heaven. Why grace in itself might be lost if it were not for the Holy Spirit that dwells in your hearts that is the fountain of it! The stream may be cut off, but if the stream has a fountain that continually bubbles up, the stream will never be dried up. The perpetuity of the stream depends upon the fountain. Now, who is the fountain of all grace? It is the Holy Spirit. 'Whoever believes in me, as the Scripture has said, "Out of his heart will flow rivers of living water"' (John 7:38). Here is a fountain from which shall flow rivers of living water. Who is this fountain? Read on: 'Now this he said about the Spirit, whom those who believed in him were to receive' (John 7:39).

It is the same Spirit who works grace and works glory. In Romans 8:23 we are said to have received the first fruits of the Spirit. Why is grace there called the first fruits of the Spirit? Because if you have the Spirit you shall have glory. The same Spirit that works grace works glory, as the same ground that bears the first fruits bears the crop. Learn therefore to value and prize this great gift of the Holy Spirit. If he dwells in you and has begun to work grace in your hearts, which is the proof that his Person is given to your persons, he will never leave you.

The Spirit does not dwell in us as he did in Adam, so long as we are holy. Instead he dwells in us to work holiness, therefore, when we are unholy. I will name just one place that shows this: 'If the Spirit of him who raised Jesus from the dead dwells in you, he who raised Christ Jesus from the dead will also give life to your mortal bodies through his Spirit who dwells in you' (Rom. 8:11). My brothers, does the Spirit dwell in you now? When you are laid in the grave the same Spirit dwells in you as dwelt in the body of Christ. I do not say in the same high manner. The Spirit of God dwelt in the body of Christ in the grave and raised it up. He never left him, though his body was a dead carcass without a soul. Yet that human body was united to the Godhead, therefore it is called 'Holy One': 'My Holy One shall not see corruption.'

Now the comparison is, if we have the Spirit of Christ and if he dwells in us, the same Spirit shall never leave our bodies till he has raised us up also. While your body is dead and rotting in the grave the Holy Spirit dwells in it. So that now the gift of the Holy Spirit is the greatest deposit of heaven that could be. That is the first way the Spirit assures us of heaven.

As the Spirit is a deposit of heaven, so the graces of the Spirit also assure us of heaven, for that is one use of a deposit. My brothers, grace is part of heaven, as I have often expressed it. He that believes has eternal life. Love, you know, is said to remain (1 Cor. 13), and grace is called the first fruits of the Spirit (Rom. 8:23). And so now in general you see how the Holy Spirit is said to be the deposit of our inheritance in a more large sense than the work of assurance. He is a deposit both in the gift of his Person and likewise in his graces.

What graces you will say? The graces of faith and love. You would look for some glorious thing now. Faith and love are the graces that God works by the Person of the Holy Spirit given to you. The Apostle instances these two in the next verse to the text: 'For this reason, because I have heard of your faith in the Lord Jesus and your love toward all the saints' (Eph. 1:15). Has the Holy Spirit produced these in your heart? These are a deposit that the Person of the Holy Spirit has given to you, and the Person of the Holy Spirit being given to you is a deposit of the inheritance that God has appointed for his children and which shall be yours. The Spirit dwelling in you that dwelt in Christ shall raise up your mortal body as it raised up Christ's.

An Assurance of Heaven in the Person of the Spirit

Now I must come to the second point and show you how the Holy Spirit is said to be the deposit of our inheritance. Yet in a more proper sense it is spoken in respect of the work of assurance which the Holy Spirit works in us.

Assurance is the particular and special thing that the Holy Spirit has in his eye. He couples it with sealing. He has sealed us by his Spirit who is the deposit, and, as a sealer, the Spirit gives assurance. We have assurance in us of our redemption. Compare Ephesians 4:30 where you read we are 'sealed for the day of redemption', meaning that God has produced assurance in us that we shall be redeemed, and he has sealed us up to the day of redemption. Here it is. He is the deposit of our inheritance until the redemption, so that both signify the work of assurance. …

Now what is deposit? It is giving you part in hand, part of that joy and comfort, that taste of heaven. When he thus seals he accompanies it with a taste of joy unspeakable and glorious. It is a part taken up beforehand as heirs take up money upon their lands beforehand. It is not a bare conviction that a man shall go to heaven, but God tells him in part what heaven is and lets the soul feel it. There is nothing sweeter than the love of God and the tasting of that sweetness in the deposit of the inheritance.

I shall now come to some observations.

Celebrate Your Safety

There is no falling from grace. Why? Because the gift of the Holy Spirit and his graces and the work of assurance are a deposit. Pledges indeed are restored again. If the Holy Spirit were only a pledge or a loan it were something; but he is also said to be a deposit. Now what says Christ? 'I will give you another Counsellor to be with you forever' (cf. John 14:16), never to be returned again, as you know a deposit is not.

The truth is this: if men to whom he gives the Spirit should not be saved, God must lose his deposit. He must lose his Spirit. As he would not lose the death of his Son so that he should die in vain, so he will not lose his Spirit whom he gives as a deposit unto believers says Christ says to Mary, 'You have chosen the better part which shall never be taken from you' (Luke 10:42).

You that have the deposit of the Spirit, prize it. You use to lay up your deposit-money by which you may sue for the bargain safely and carefully. You prize it more than all your other money, as you do your bonds more than all your other papers in your study, because you have that to sue for your debt. Value therefore the Holy Spirit's graces, especially the deposit of him whereby he works assurance.

Enjoy the Love of God

See the love of God, that God should not only bestow an inheritance upon us, but bestow himself upon us for himself. He not only makes us heirs of himself, but makes us his own inheritance too, for this is what is meant by the word 'possession'. For God who is blessed for ever and needs no creature should call his people his inheritance which he lives upon, as it were. For you know that a man's inheritance is that he lives upon and calls his purchased possession.

Here was love, that he should purchase this inheritance by the blood of Christ and pay so dear for it. They are not only his inheritance, but his purchased inheritance too. He did it to show his love the more.

When he had bought us by Christ he shows yet a further love. For though we were bought and the price was paid, we still lie in sins, and therefore he sends his Spirit into our hearts to rescue us, to subdue us and to redeem us until the redemption of the purchased possession he gives the Spirit as a deposit.

He gives us this Spirit as a deposit to assure us in the meantime and to comfort us. He not only reserves heaven for us as it is (1 Pet. 1:4), but he is careful to give us the Comforter while we are here.

Set Your Heart on the Glory of Heaven

Heaven is an inheritance given to us, and God's inheritance. Great men give inheritances answerable to their greatness; what inheritance then will God give himself, as you heard before? As heirs of God and co-heirs with Christ you cannot be more happy than God can make you or than Jesus Christ is. And you are co-heirs with him.

How great must that inheritance be when joy in the Holy Spirit is but the deposit! The deposit you know is but part in hand. It is what but a sixpence may be to a thousand pounds. How great is the possession when the deposit is so great! Take joy in the Holy Spirit, which fills your hearts fuller of joy than all the good things in the world will do. As David tells you, it is more than corn and wine and oil (Psa. 4:7). Are you in distress? It carries you above all those distresses. We rejoice in our sufferings, says the Apostle (Rom. 5:3). Rejoice, James says, when you fall into all sorts of trials (James 1:2). This the Holy Spirit does. If the deposit does this (and a little piece of it at that), then what will the possession itself be?

The great inheritance is to come. It is called the purchased possession if you take it to refer to heaven. Purchased by what? By the blood of Christ. What do you think the purchase of Christ's blood is worth? Consider that 'a king's ransom' is used to express a great sum. What will the ransom be that was made by the blood, a ransom so the text says (1 Tim. 2:6)? What will the ransom by the blood of God come to, when Jesus Christ laid down his blood? Christ says, 'Let my heirs take out all that blood of mine in glory and grace.' What will that glory come to?

It is both a redemption and a possession. Two things in hell make men miserable, and divines know not which is the greater. The one is the anguish of loss, that they have lost heaven and happiness and that torments them. The other is the anguish of feeling, the feeling of the wrath of God. The glory of heaven which makes us happy also consists of two things: a redemption from misery and the possession of happiness.

To the Praise of His Glory

There is yet one thing more in the text of which I must speak, and they are the last words in the fourteenth verse, 'to the praise of his glory'. It is a thing mentioned as the purpose of all. It is mentioned in the sixth verse as the purpose of election, 'to the praise of His glorious grace'. It is mentioned in the 12th verse in his application to the Jews, that we should be to the praise of his glory, who first trusted in Christ. It is mentioned here again in the 14th verse, when he makes application of all to the Gentiles, 'in whom you also trusted, to the praise of his glory'. You shall find that in all the enumerations of the benefits of God towards us these two things come in again and again, in Christ and to the praise of his glory. 'In Christ' comes nine times; 'to the praise of His glory' comes three times. There is a trinity of glory to God, as there are Three Persons whom he has distinctly mentioned as the authors of our salvation, both God the Father and God the Son in whom we have redemption through his blood (at the 7th verse) and God the Holy Spirit, 'by whom you are sealed who is the deposit of our inheritance' (cf. Eph. 1:13-14).

'To the praise of his glory' refers first to the persons when Paul spoke of the salvation of the Jews (Eph. 1:11-12). There he mentions their salvation to be to the praise of God's glory. When he speaks it again to the Gentiles he sounds it out again: to the praise of his glory. God is exceedingly glorified when the Gentiles are added to the Church. So it is said in Acts that when they saw that God had given repentance to the Gentiles, they glorified God (Acts 11:18). And in making reference both to the Jew and Gentile he distinctly mentions 'to the praise of his glory'. He states that in the conclusion of his application to the Jew (Eph. 1:12) as well as in the conclusion of his application to the Gentile (Eph. 1:14). As it refers thus to the persons that God should have glory for converting. Likewise, it refers to the special benefits he has mentioned. He has mentioned their believing, their being sealed, and their having the Holy Spirit as a deposit of their inheritance to the praise of his glory.

Every new benefit should have 'to the praise of his glory' added to it in our hearts. Do you believe? Live to the praise of his glory. Have you assurance added to your faith and a being sealed by the Holy Spirit of promise? There is a further expectation that you should be to the praise of his glory, for God is committed to that, if you are sealed and glorified. He that is sealed for the day of salvation and has joy unspeakable and glorious, has not only his heart filled with the Spirit of grace, but, as the Apostle says (1 Pet. 4:14), he has the Spirit of glory resting on him. He has the beginnings of glory in his heart. Therefore it is expected that he should live much more to God's glory.

Further Reading

- Thomas Goodwin, *The Heart of Christ* (Edinburgh: Banner of Truth, 2011).

- Thomas Goodwin, *Christ Set Forth: As the Cause of Justification and as the Object of Justifying Faith* (Edinburgh: Banner of Truth, 2015).

- Joel Beeke & Mark Jones (eds.), *A Habitual Sight of Him: The Christ-Centered Piety of Thomas Goodwin* (Grand Rapids: Reformation Heritage Books, 2009).

- *The Works of Thomas Goodwin*, 12 vols. (Grand Rapids: Reformation Heritage Books, 2001).

3

SAMUEL RUTHERFORD
on Covenant Confidence

I N 1650 an English businessman was returning from a trip to Scotland. He told a friend that he had heard three preachers there. One showed him the majesty of God, another 'showed me all my heart', and then 'I heard a little fair man, and he showed me the loveliness of Christ'. That man was Samuel Rutherford (1600–1661), and his skill in showing the loveliness of Jesus Christ, in the depths of theology and in the heights of personal devotion, is the reason why we should get to know and read him.

Born in the Scottish Borders, he went to the University of Edinburgh where his gifts were quickly recognized, and he was given a teaching position after graduating in 1623. All looked set for an academic career, but Rutherford's life was thrown into upheaval. It seems likely that Rutherford got his wife-to-be, Eupham, pregnant. Whether or not this was the 'great scandal' to which he later alluded, something broke Rutherford, forcing him to leave Edinburgh, and he was quite possibly converted to Christ as a result.

His repentance must have been sincere, because just a year later he began parish ministry in the tiny village of Anwoth in south-west Scotland. Maybe an enduring sense of shame made him go far from Edinburgh and accept a meagre salary. The Lord was in it, though, and the years at Anwoth, while full of trials (including the death of Eupham and two of their children), were years of fruitful ministry.

Rutherford was a man of strong convictions which would set him on a collision course with the church powers of his day. As his preaching and writing ministry gained more influence, so did opposition. And in 1636 Rutherford was exiled to Aberdeen because of his non-conformity. Although saddened by the loss of friends and his ministry, he resolved to use his prison days well, and letters and other works followed.

Two years later King Charles I and Archbishop William Laud tried to impose a new liturgy on the Scots. A National Covenant was signed by those who opposed the King and this was adopted by the Scottish Parliament in 1640. Soon both Scotland and England were embroiled in civil war. Rutherford was given a position at the University of St Andrews, where he went with extreme reluctance, as he was so attached to his Anwoth people. He stayed for the next twelve years, teaching, writing and preaching.

Rutherford's reputation is centred on two strikingly different works. The first is the collection of his letters. These were written over the course of many years to a range of correspondents, including members of the Scottish gentry supportive of the Christian faith in the nation. Rutherford gives counsel, reassurance, warning and encouragement in all manner of life situations. As well as giving us fascinating insights into the friendships and trials of seventeenth-century people, the letters frequently soar to heights of devotion to Christ. Rutherford spoke of his love for Christ with language which is at times (to our modern tastes) alarmingly erotic and highly subjective. And yet his prose still has the power to thrill us with the truths that Jesus loves us and wants us to discover that love in greater measure.

The Victorian preacher Charles Spurgeon called the letters 'the nearest thing to inspiration which can be found in all the writings of mere men'. They reveal the heart-life of a man who loved Christ ardently. Rutherford knew sorrow and joy, and he felt life very deeply. When he writes to friends suffering bereavement, doubt and temptation, he writes with transparent concern, and gives a word of sure and loving authority to help them. Seventeenth-century life was hard, uncertain and usually short. But Rutherford was fixed on the world to come, heart and soul. Most of all, he was fixed on its King, the Lord Jesus. His letters breathe this conviction: 'Oh, that He would fold the heavens together like an old cloak, and shovel time and days out of the way, and make ready in haste the Lamb's wife for her Husband! Since He looked upon me, my heart is not mine own; He hath run away to heaven with it.'

As well as being an insightful pastor, Rutherford was also a brilliant theologian. His second landmark work *Lex Rex*, 'The Law and the King' (1644), is a masterpiece of political theology. The book marshals the revealed law of God and God's natural order in order to undercut the ambitions of King Charles I as head of the church and to bolster the claims of Scottish Presbyterianism. *Lex Rex* had seismic effect in its century and beyond, giving strength to armed resistance against the Crown in Scotland. It also helped to form the thinking behind the American and French Revolutions of the following century. *Lex Rex* was one of over a dozen theological works which, when added to sermons, tracts, commentaries and letters, almost match John Owen's output in scale and importance. Rutherford was also one of the framers of the Westminster Standards.

After the restoration of the monarchy, Rutherford was ordered to answer for his views in *Lex Rex*. He knew he would be condemned and likely sentenced to death. He also knew that he answered to a higher Court and served a great King. As it happened, illness meant Rutherford died in 1661 before the trial could begin.

What to Look Out For

The Trial and Triumph of Faith is a series of twenty-seven sermons on the exchange between Christ and the Syro-Phoeni-
cian woman, recorded in Matthew 15:21-28 and Mark 7:24-30.
Rutherford explores the person of Christ, the nature of grace
and the character of saving faith. He opens up the wells of
rich, sound theology, while painting a vivid portrait of the
saving work of God in bringing hungry and thirsty sinners
to Christ.

This sermon below (number seven) shows how Rutherford
brings his theological mind to bear on our everyday struggles of faith. Showing us how God's dealings with us are all
through Christ, our Covenant-Head, Rutherford explores how
loved and safe we are in him. As Rutherford says, 'It is full of
comfort for us that the Father and Christ transacted a bargain
from eternity concerning you by name.' The sermon is an invitation to understand that 'bargain' and to explore its comforts.

�֎

The Trial and Triumph of Faith

From Sermon Seven[1]

Christ was a King by the covenant of grace and the special
party of the new covenant. This may be made more evident
if we enquire a little into the covenant:

1. What it is.

2. Who are the parties.

3. What are its promises.

---

[1] Samuel Rutherford, *The Trial and Triumph of Faith* (Edinburgh: Banner of
Truth, 2007), pp. 73-85.

What is the Covenant?

1. The covenant is here a joint and mutual bargain between two parties, according to which they promise freely such and such things each to other. In this case God and man made up a solemn bargain in Christ.

2. Both parties consent. Christ did not force his spouse to marry against her will, nor was God forced to make a covenant. Love and grace were what led Christ's hand to the pen in signing the covenant with his blood.

3. As a cluster of stars makes a constellation and a body of branches a tree, so a mass of promises come from this covenant. Wherever Christ is, clusters of divine promises grow out of him as the rays and beams from the sun, and a family (as it were) and a society of branches out of a tree.

4. There is here giving and receiving. Christ offers and gives such and such favours, and we receive all by believing, except the grace of faith itself which cannot be received by faith, but which is given freely and graciously by God. Grace, first and last, was all our happiness. If there had not been a Saviour (to borrow that expression) made all of grace, grace itself, we could never have had dealings with God.

Who Is the Covenant Made Between?

The parties of the covenant are God and man. Oh how sweet that such a potter and such a former of all things should come to make a bargain with such clay as is guilty before him! Now the parties here on the one part is God, on the other the Mediator Christ, along with the children that the Lord gave him. Observe that in the covenant of nature and works God and his friend Adam were the parties making the contract. And in the second covenant God and his fellow Christ and all his are the parties. A covenant of peace cannot be made between an enemy and an enemy. Those who were enemies must lay down their wrath before they can enter into a covenant. Contrary parties, as contrary parties, cannot be united. So God being the sole author of this covenant laid aside enmity first. Love must first send out love as fire must cast out heat. It is true this covenant is made with sinners (just as God made the covenant of nature with Adam when he was still righteous), but a covenant union could never have been, except God had in a manner bowed to us and grace proved out of measure gracious.

As Christ is the key party here, so Christ has a sevenfold relationship to the covenant.

1. Christ Is the Covenant Itself

Christ is the Covenant itself. 'I will give you as a covenant for the people, a light for the nations' (Isa 42:6). 'I will keep you and give you as a covenant to the people' (Isa. 49:8). Christ, God and man is all the covenant, both because he is given to fulfil the covenant on both sides, and because he is the covenant in the abstract. He is very peace and reconciliation itself. 'And this man shall be the peace when the Assyrian shall come into our land' (cf. Mic. 5:5). As fire is hot for itself and all things hot with it, so by participation you are so far in covenant with Christ as you have everything that belongs to Christ. Lack Christ, and you lack peace and the covenant.

2. Christ Is the Messenger of the Covenant

As Christ deals between the parties, he is the Messenger of the covenant. 'And the Lord whom you seek will suddenly come to his temple; and the messenger of the covenant in whom you delight' (Mal. 3:1). Christ travels with tidings between the parties. He reports of God to us, 'that it is his Father's will that we be saved' (cf. John 6:39). Christ reports of himself, for it sets Christ to be a broker for Christ and Wisdom to cry in the streets: 'Who will have me?' (cf. Prov. 1:20, 22; 9:1-5). It became the Lord Jesus to praise himself: 'I am the Bread of life, I am the Light of the world' (John 6:48; 8:12). 'I am the door' (10:9), and 'I am the good Shepherd' (verse 11). He praises his Father: 'My Father is the gardener' (cf. John 15:1). He suits us in marriage, and commends his Father: You marry me, dear souls; oh but my Father is a great person. 'In my Father's house are many rooms' (John 14:2). He commends us to the Father as a messenger making peace would do: 'For I have given them the words that you gave me, and they have received them and have come to know in truth that I came from you; and they have believed that you sent me' (John 17:8). 'O righteous Father, even though the world does not know you, I know you, and these know that you have sent me' (verse 25). Ministers cannot speak of Christ and his Father as he can do himself. Oh come, hear Christ speak of Christ and of his Father, and of heaven, for he saw all.

3. Christ Is the Witness of the Covenant

As Christ saw and heard and testifies all, he is the Witness of the covenant. The whole covenant was a bloody act acted upon his person. Behold, I have given him for a witness to the people (Isa. 55:4), the faithful Witness (Rev. 1:5), the Amen, the faithful and true Witness (Rev. 3:14). The covenant says that 'The Son of Man came to seek and to save the lost' (Luke 19:10). 'Amen', says Christ, 'I can witness that to be true.' Christ died and rose again for sinners. 'Amen', says the Witness, 'I was dead and behold I live for evermore' (cf. Rev. 1:18). 'Amen', Christ puts his seal to that. 'The saying is trustworthy and deserving of full acceptance, that Christ Jesus came into the

world to save sinners' (1 Tim. 1:15). 'I can swear that is true',
says Christ. The world shall have an end (says the covenant),
and time shall be no more. 'By him who lives for ever and
ever, who created heaven and earth', says this angel witness
(Rev. 10:6). That is most true, time shall be no more. Christ
shall judge the world and all shall bow to him. This Amen of
God says that is true, for it is written, 'as I live, says the Lord,
every knee shall bow to me', (Rom. 14:11). The covenant of
works had a promise, but, because it was both conditional
and to be broken and done away with, it had no oath of God
as this has. O doubting soul, you say that your salvation is not
sure. 'Alas', you say, 'God loves not me'. Have you the Son?
You have a true testimony that it is not so, and 'a faithful witness does not lie' (Prov. 14:5). Christ has cause to remember
that you are saved. He bears the marks of it in his body. Athe-
ist, you say, 'Who knows if there is a heaven and a hell?' Why,
the witness of the covenant says, 'I was in both and saw both'.

4. Christ Is the Guarantee of the Covenant

As he undertakes for the parties in conflict, Christ is the
Guarantee of the covenant. Christ is the guarantee of the
better covenant (Heb. 7:22) and in this the Father is guarantee for Christ. If he undertakes for David and Hezekiah (Psa.
119:122, Isa. 38:14), far more for his own Son. God has given
his word for Christ, that he shall do the work: 'Behold, my
servant shall act wisely' (Isa. 52:13) and 'Behold, the Lord GOD
helps me' (Isa. 50:9). And again, the Son is guarantee to the
Father and the great undertaker that God the Father shall
fulfil his part of the covenant to give a kingdom to his flock
(Luke 12:32; John 6:37, 39).

Christ, as guarantee for us, has paid a ransom for us. He
gives a new heart to his fellow confederates [those in covenant with him]. He is engaged to lose none of them (John

17:12), but raise them up at the last day (John 6:39). If we could surrender ourselves to Christ's undertaking and get a word that he is a guarantee to the Father for us, all would be well. Woe to the foolish man, as he has not Christ under an act and bond of guarantee that he shall keep him to the day of God. We make foolish bargains on behalf of our souls.

5. Christ Is the Mediator of the Covenant

As he stands between the contrary parties, Christ is the Mediator of the covenant (Heb. 12:24). He is Mediator by virtue of who he is. Our text calls him 'Lord' and 'the Son of David'. By condition of nature he has something of God, as being true God, and something of man, as sharing with us. He is also mediator by office and lays his hands on both parties as a mediator does (Job 9:33). In this he has a threefold relationship:

1. Firstly, he is a friend to both, as he has God's heart for man to be gracious and satisfy mercy, and a man's heart for God to satisfy justice.

2. Secondly, he is a reconciler, to make two one, to bring down God to a treaty of peace, and to take him and the high demands and condemnation of law, which sought personal satisfaction of us, and in his body to bring us up to God by a ransom paid, and by giving us faith to draw near to his Father. So he may say, 'Sister and spouse, come up now to my Father and your Father, to my God and your God; and Father, come down to my brothers, my kindred and flesh'.

3. And thirdly, he is a common servant to both. He was God's servant in as hard piece of service as ever was: 'Behold, my servant' (Isa. 52:13; 42:1) and 'My righteous servant' (cf. Isa. 53:11). And our servant for he 'came

not to be served but to serve, and to give his life as a ransom for many' (Matt. 20:28).

Alas, both parties struck him. It pleased the Lord to bruise him (Isa. 53:10). God spared not his own Son (Rom. 8:32). And the other party (his own) struck him. 'This is the heir; come, let us kill him,' they say, 'and seize the inheritance' (Matt. 21:38). This was cold encouragement to sweet Jesus. If it had been referred to us, for shame, we could not have asked God to be a suffering Mediator for us. There is more love in Christ than angels and men could fathom in their conceptions.

6. Christ Is the Signatory of the Covenant

As he signs the covenant and signs off all its articles, he is the Testator or Signatory of the covenant. The covenant is the testament of our dead friend Jesus: he died to confirm the testament (Heb. 9:16-17). No other blood could seal the covenant, but Christ's blood, as dying, sealed the everlasting covenant (Heb. 13:20). It both expiated the sins of the covenanters and also brought back the great Shepherd of the sheep from death. For, Christ having once paid blood and died, it guaranteed our release from prison, when he had paid the sum.

7. Christ Is the Party of the Covenant

Christ is the party contracting in the covenant, representing both sides. For here Christ comes under a double consideration, one as God, so he is one with the Father and Spirit and the Lord, and the author of the covenant, and then as Mediator he is on our side of the covenant. So the covenant was made with Christ and all his heirs and assignees, principally with Christ and with Abraham's nature in him, but also personally with each believer. So Christ the heir of all things and the second heirs under him [believers] are all one covenant family. The covenant made with David and his seed and the fathers is fulfilled to Christ and his seed. As concerning that he raised him up from the dead no more to see corruption, he said, 'I will give you the holy and sure blessings of David' (Acts 13:34). As the covenant of nature and works was made with Adam and all his, and there were not two covenants, so here the better covenant coming in place of the former is made with the second Adam and his children (Rom. 5:18-19, 1 Cor. 15:20-22).

All that is required to make a covenant are here. First, God demands of his Son that he lay down his life; and for his labour he promises, 'that he shall see his seed and God shall give him many children' (cf. Isa. 53:10). Second, the Son consents to lay down his life and says, 'Here am I to do your will. You have given me a body.' This is the formality of a covenant, when Christ consents to the condition.

Now this covenant was manifested in time between the Father and the Son, but it was transacted from eternity. It is full of comfort for us that the Father and Christ transacted a bargain from eternity concerning you by name. There was communing between the Father and Son concerning your heaven. 'Father, what shall be given to your justice to ransom one such as John, Anna etc.?' And Christ from eternity covenanted for such a person as you so that you should believe in time. The redemption of sinners is not a work of yesterday or a business of chance. It was well advised and in infinite wisdom contrived. Therefore do not grieve Christ by refusing the gospel. When you believe, you make Christ's word good. He that believes not makes God a liar.

Men believe the gospel to be a cunningly devised fable (2 Pet. 1:16). The Father and Christ are both in this business; heaven, hell, justice, mercy, souls and deep wisdom are all in this rare piece, and yet men think more of a farm and an ox (Luke 14:18-19) and of a pin in the state, or a straw, or of the bones of a crazy livelihood, or a house.

What Are the Covenant Promises?

There is no good thing which is not ours by free promise, and not by simple donation only. This covenant turns over heaven, earth, sea, land, bread, garments, sleep, the world, life, and death into free grace. Indeed, it makes sin and crosses, golden sins, and crosses by accident through the acts of supernatural providence towards us (1 Cor. 3:21; Rom. 8:28), working on and about our sins.

All good comes to us now, not immediately, but through the hands of a free Redeemer. Although he is a man who redeemed us, yet because he is also God there is more of God and heaven and free love in all our good things than if we received them immediately from God, as ravens have their food from God without a mediator, and devils have their being only by creature-right, not by covenant-right.

As for the promises, they flow from God to us, but all along they fall first on Christ. They are of two sorts: some are only given to Christ and not to us. These include the promise that his name will be adored above all names. To be set at the right hand of God is properly promised only to Christ. Angels do not share with him in this chair (Phil. 2:9-10; Heb. 1:5, 13). There is promised to Christ a seed, a willing people, and the ends of the earth for his inheritance (Isa. 53:10; Psa. 10:2; 2:8-9).

There are also other promises which come to Christ's seed along with Christ. These are of two types, general and specific.

The General Promise

The mother promise that 'I will be your God' is made to Christ. He shall cry to me, 'You are my Father, my God' (Psa. 89:26). But it is also made to us, 'I will be your God' (cf. John 20:17; Psa. 22:1). How sweet is it that Christ, having God as his Father by eternal birth-right, would take a new covenant-right to God for our cause. Oh what an honour it is to be within the covenant with the first Heir.

But why are all the promises enclosed in this one, 'I will be your God'? Here is the answer: because Christ has covenant-right to the promises by this chief right, that God is his God by covenant. And so, we first must have God made ours in a covenant as a Father and a Husband. Only then, by law, does all that he possesses become ours. Christ himself is more than grace, pardon, holiness—more than created glory. As the husband is more excellent than his marriage robe, bracelets and rings, so we are to lay our love and faith principally upon the Father and the Son more than all the created gifts they give. The well and fountain of life is more excellent than the streams, and the tree of life than the apples. As the tree of life Christ himself, the objective happiness, is far above a created blessing which issues from him just as the whole is more excellent than the part, and the cause more excellent than the effect.

The Specific Promises

Special promises are made first to Christ and then by proportion to us and they are these:

1. God promises to grace his Son above his fellows, that he may die and suffer and so merit a corresponding grace for us which is this: a new heart and a new spirit (Jer. 32:39; Ezek. 36:26-27). For out of his fullness we receive grace for grace (John 1:16).

2. Justification is promised to Christ, not personally, as if he needed a pardon for sin. But because of his work, there is a righteousness guaranteed, due to the guarantee when he has paid the debts of the broken man, who comes out of prison free by law. So he came out of the grave for our righteousness, but having first the righteousness of his cause in his own person. 'He who vindicates me is near', says Christ, 'who will contend

with me?' (Isa. 50:8). He was 'vindicated by the Spirit' (1 Tim. 3:16). So have we justification of our persons and remission in his blood (Eph. 1:7), and that through the covenant (Jer. 31:32-33).

3. Victory and dominion are promised to Christ (Psa. 110:1-2, Psa. 89:21). 'He must reign till he has put all his enemies under his feet' (1 Cor. 15:25) and so victory over all our enemies is promised to us (John 16:33; 14:30; Rom. 6:14-15; Gal. 3:13; Col. 2:14-15).

4. The kingdom and glory is sought by Christ (John 17:5) from his Father. And he had a word of promise from his Father for it (Phil 2:9-10) and we have that also (Luke 12:32; John 17:24; 14:1-3).

5. Christ had a word of promise when he went down to the grave, as someone might go to prison having in his bosom from his prince a bill of grace that within three days he shall come out to enjoy all his previous honours and court (Psa. 16:10-11). This is what we have in Christ (John 11:26; 6:38-39).

Further Reading

- Samuel Rutherford, *The Trial and Triumph of Faith* (Edinburgh: Banner of Truth, 2007).

- *The Letters of Samuel Rutherford: A Selection* (Edinburgh: Banner of Truth, 2015).

- Samuel Rutherford, *The Loveliness of Christ* (Edinburgh: Banner of Truth, 2007).

- Faith Cook, *Samuel Rutherford and His Friends*, (Edinburgh: Banner of Truth, 2013).

4

WILLIAM BRIDGE
on Suffering

T HE Puritans not only diligently studied God's word,
they also studied human beings. And their ability to
make the connection between theology and the concerns of
their congregations produced a wealth of rich pastoral writings. In addition to the clarity of their God-centred vision,
this is a key reason why they are still valued today. Their
reflections on suffering in the light of God's providence are a
resource to treasure. *A Lifting Up for the Downcast* by William
Bridge (1600–1670) is a great example of this.

Bridge's faith and learning were nurtured in Cambridge
University, which he entered as a sixteen year old, and stayed
on as a teacher until in his thirties. He then accepted a pastorate in Norwich before being forced into exile in Amsterdam during a period when Archbishop Laud made life all but
impossible for Puritans. Bridge returned to England in 1642
where he participated in the Westminster Assembly, where he
was another clear and persuasive voice for the Independents.
His preaching was highly valued, and almost all of his work
which has remained are sermons. Bridge became a pastor in
Great Yarmouth, before again being forced from the ministry
during the Great Ejection of 1662. His last years were spent
pastoring just outside London. Like so many gospel servants of his age, Bridge knew great personal upheaval in his

allegiance to Christ. As one shaped by his sufferings Bridge is an able guide to us as we seek grace in our own trials.

What to Look Out For

A Lifting Up for the Downcast was originally delivered as sermons. As the title suggests, Bridge provides counsel for despondent Christians. Our first extract is taken from the introductory sermon in which Bridge, building on the foundation of God's sovereignty, explains how God both provides comfort in difficult circumstances and uses them for his purposes.

Bridge then addresses a number of specific case studies. Our second extract is taken from his sermon on those facing external affliction. 'But now that these stinging bees and wasps flock about you,' he says, 'what does this prove but that you have got some honey, something that tastes good and of Christ, which you did not have before. Why should you not therefore rather praise God for what you have, than be discouraged by the opposition you face?'[1]

Bridge deals with people who claim it's different for them. These are people who agree with Bridge in principle that comfort can be found in afflictions, but see themselves as an exception. He also imagines someone complaining that their afflictions have stopped them serving Christ. Bridge replies that affliction may be God's call to another way of serving Christ. 'When God leads a man into an affliction, then God calls him to another work ... It may be your affliction may hinder you from your former work which God has called you from, but it does not hinder you from that work to which you are now called by your affliction.'[2]

---

[1] William Bridge, *A Lifting Up for the Downcast* (Edinburgh: Banner of Truth, 2009), p. 202.

[2] *Ibid.*, pp. 202-203.

❊

A Lifting Up for the Downcast

Sermon 3—Saints Should Not Be Discouraged, Whatever Their Condition Be[3]

> Why are you cast down, O my soul,
>
> and why are you in turmoil within me?
>
> Hope in God; for I shall again praise him,
>
> my salvation and my God.
>
> *Psalm 42:11*

What should I do ... that I may not be discouraged, whatever my condition? The only way which the Psalmist teaches here is to hope, trust, believe in God. Here are six directions on how we should use our faith in Christ so that we may not be discouraged.

1. Find Encouragement in God Rather Than Your Circumstances

If you want to avoid being discouraged in any condition, then never link your comforts to your condition, nor be in love with any condition for itself. Don't let your condition itself be the cause or foundation of your encouragements. Hang a cloak or garment upon a rotten peg, and the peg will break and the garment will fall. Now there is no condition that is not like a rotten peg. Every condition is alterable. No condition is so firm and fast that is not exposed to many changes or to a rotten hold. God, however, is a pillar. Indeed, he is many pillars. His name is *Adonai* (Lord) which signifies so much. In Isaiah 26:4 we are commanded to trust in the Lord, 'for in the Lord Jehovah is everlasting strength.' He is 'the Rock of Ages'. Says

---

[3] Bridge, *Lifting Up*, pp. 62-66.

the Psalmist, 'My flesh and my heart may fail, but God is the strength of my heart and my portion forever' (Psa. 73:26). If you lay your comforts upon your own condition, then you build on the sand. Such comforts will be carried away with every wind and storm and tempest. But if you build upon Christ himself and upon God himself then you build upon the Rock. And, though the floods and storms and winds rise and beat upon you, yet you shall not lose your comforts because they are built upon a rock.

2. Make Links Between Your Circumstances and Christ

Be sure that you think of Christ in a right way and manner as he suits your condition and as he is held forth in the gospel. We are very apt to have mis-thoughts of Christ. Just as Satan transforms himself into an angel of light, so Satan would transform Christ before you into an angel of darkness. But the Scriptures hold forth the person of Christ in ways that make him very amiable to poor sinners:

- Are you accused by Satan, the world or your own conscience? He is called your Advocate.

- Are you ignorant? He is called the Prophet.

- Are you guilty of sin? He is called a Priest and High Priest.

- Are you afflicted with many enemies, inward and outward? He is called a King, and King of kings.

- Are you in dire straits? He is called your Way.

- Are you hungry or thirsty? He is called the Bread and Water of Life.

- Are you afraid you shall fall away and be condemned at the last? He is our second Adam, our representative, in whose death we died and in whose satisfaction we satisfied God's requirements.

Just as there is no temptation or affliction, but some promise or other is especially suited to it, so there is no condition, but some name, some title, some attribute of Christ is especially suited to it. So you should not just look on Christ, but make the link to your condition. And, in the same way, you are not to look upon your condition alone, but match it with a suitable attribute of Christ. If you look upon Christ's attribute of love without looking at your condition, you may presume. If you look on your condition without looking at Christ's attribute of love, you may despair. Think on both together and you will not be discouraged.

3. Avoid Being Introspective

If your discouragements begin to arise and press in upon you, check yourself, and say:

> Why should I multiply thoughts without knowledge? Why should I tire out my soul with these thoughts? Am I able to add one cubit to my spiritual state? Am I, by all my thoughtfulness, able to alter my condition? In fact, does not my thoughtfulness set me at a farther distance from the mercy desired?

The truth is that the only way to lose the comfort you desire is to be anxious about it. Often the only way to have an outward blessing is to be content to go without it. In the same way, the only way to have a spiritual or outward affliction removed is to be content that it should be continued if God and Christ will have it so. But you say you must have your affliction immediately removed, and you must immediately know that you are in the state of grace and the child of God— or else you will be discouraged. You are like the bird in the net: the more it strives, the more it is entangled. Suppose temptations, afflictions and desertions come, and Satan adds to them by saying to your soul, 'This will always be'? Answer like this:

Well, I therefore believe the opposite because you say it, Satan, and you are a liar. Yet if God will have it so, I am contented. I leave it to him. Whether I shall always be in this condition or not is not my question. But now, O Lord, let me serve you. That is all my desire. Let me see you as you please and when you please. I have done, Lord, I have done. I have been questioning and questioning my condition for many years. I see there is no end of that. Indeed, the more I do it, the more I get nothing by it. Why, therefore, oh my soul, should I tear out myself with this kind of thoughtfulness?

Check yourselves like this.

4. Consider the Sweetness That Accompanies Difficult Circumstances

Whenever you think of anything which is in itself terrible, or a matter of discouragement, be sure that you mingle the consideration of it with those sweet things which God has given and prescribed to you. There is nothing terrible, but God has joined some comfort with it. The name of God is terrible, for he is called the great and dreadful God. But to sweeten this he is also called the God of all consolations. Death is terrible. It is called the king of terrors. But to sweeten this, it is called a sleep. The day of judgment is terrible. But to sweeten that, our present Advocate shall be our future Judge; yes, our best Friend and our dear Husband. Now if you separate the terror of any object from its sweetness, no wonder you are much discouraged. It is our duty to behold things as God presents them and to take things as God gives them. What God has joined together, no man may put asunder. If you consider the sweetness of an object or condition, without the sourness of it, then you may grow too lax. If you consider the terror of an object or condition, without the sweetness of it, then you may be too fearful. But if you think on both together then you will fear and believe, and believe and fear—and so be kept from discouragement.

5. Put to Death Self-Love

If you would not be discouraged whatever your condition be, labour more and more to get your self-love mortified (put to death), even religious self-love. All your discouragements come from self-love, not from the venom of your condition, but from the poison of self-love. 'Oh,' you say, 'but I am discouraged because I have no assurance.' Well, suppose you had assurance, what then? 'Then I should have comfort,' you say, and is this not self-love? 'Oh,' you say, 'but I am discouraged about my everlasting condition.' And is not that self-love? Does not that word *condition* indicate self-love? I dare boldly say, there is no turmoil or immoderate discouragement in the soul which does not have self at the bottom. If I could I leave myself, and my condition, with God and Christ, and instead give my attention to his service, glory and honour more, then God would take care of my comfort. But when I give much of my attention to myself and my condition so much, and little of my attention to his service, glory and honour, then no wonder that I am so much discouraged. Therefore, labour more and more to mortify self-love. In this way you shall never be discouraged, whatever your condition be.

6. Don't Succumb to Doubts of Which You Will Have to Repent

In case temptation presses in upon you, and urges you to sad discouragements, speak this to your own soul: 'Why should I buy my repentance at so dear a rate?' There is none of all these doubtings, unbelieving fears and discouragements which you will not be ashamed and repent of afterwards. You know how it is with the traveller. He thinks the sun is not yet up. And so he loiters and sits down. But the sun, creeping up behind the cloud at last breaks out upon his face and is there before him. And then he says, 'O what a fool I was to think the sun was not up, just because I didn't see it. What an unwise man I was to loiter and sit down!' So it will be with you. You now lie down upon the earth and your belly cleaves to the dust because of your discouragements. But the grace of God and the love of Christ is creeping up behind the dark cloud. And it will eventually break out upon you and shine into your face with the golden beams of mercy. It will go before you and be before you. And then you will say:

> Oh what a fool I was to be so discouraged. What an unworthy creature I am to doubt God's love in this way. I have sinned. I have sinned by all my unbelief. Now, O Lord, pardon all my doubtings. I am, O Lord, ashamed of my doubtings and questionings of your love. Pardon them, O Lord, unto my soul.

This is what you must come to. In the end you will be ashamed and repent of these your unbeliefs, doubtings and fears. And therefore whenever temptation presses in on you, say *at the beginning* to yourself, 'Why should I buy my repentance at so dear a rate, by yielding to these discouragements?' And for this very reason, because discouragements are to be repented of, therefore the saints and people of God have no reason to be discouraged, whatever their condition be.

Sermon 10—A Lifting Up in the Case of Affliction[4]

Sometimes the discouragements of the saints are from their outward afflictions. I grant it is no new thing for God's own children to be much afflicted. 'These are the ones coming out of the great tribulation' (Rev. 7:14). And when God's people are so afflicted, they are very aware of their affliction. In

---

[4] Bridge, *Lifting Up*, pp. 192-198.

some respects they are more aware than wicked men. For the saints, in the day of their affliction, are more apprehensive of God's displeasure than wicked men are, and so in some respects are more aware of their afflictions.

But now I say, let a man's afflictions be ever so great, if he is in Christ and has made his peace with God, he has no reason to be cast down or discouraged, whatever his afflictions be. For our Saviour says, 'In the world you will have tribulation. But take heart; I have overcome the world' (John 16:33) … But this truth will be clear if you consider:

1.   What the afflictions and sufferings of the saints are.

2.   Where they come from.

3.   What accompanies them.

4.   What follows them, and what is achieved by them.

1. Our Afflictions Are Christ's Purchase, God's Gift and Only Apparent Evils

First, Our Afflictions are Christ's Purchase For Us

Look at Paul's inventory in 1 Corinthians 3:21-22: 'For all things are yours, whether Paul or Apollos or Cephas or the world or life or death or the present or the future'. So death itself, the king of terrors and afflictions, is here reckoned among the goods and chattels which Christ has purchased for you and left to you. And if death is yours, then all afflictions are yours and who needs to be afraid of that which is his own?

Second, Our Afflictions are the Gift of God

'For it has been granted to you that for the sake of Christ you should not only believe in him but also suffer for his sake', says the Apostle (Phil. 1:29). It was the speech of a good man, now in heaven, who was once under great afflictions. He was able to say 'O Lord, these afflictions are your pearls, and I will wear them for your sake.'

Third, Our Afflictions Only Seem Like Evils

They are real trials and seem like evils. Therefore the Apostle says, 'For the moment all discipline seems painful rather than pleasant' (Heb. 12:11). But considered altogether, it is a *seeming* grief rather than a *real* grief. Therefore Paul says, 'As unknown, and yet well known; as dying, and behold, we live; as punished, and yet not killed; as sorrowful, yet always rejoicing; as poor, yet making many rich; as having nothing, yet possessing everything' (2 Cor. 6:9-10). In which words, as Augustine observes, he puts a 'so to speak' and an 'as it were' upon his afflictions. It is as if his sufferings were *as* afflictions, but not real afflictions!

When a man takes medicine, it may make him sick. But, because they are the side-effects of medicine, you do not call it the illness. It is *like* an illness, but *not* the illness itself. Now all the afflictions of the saints are but their medicine, prescribed and given them by the hand of their Father. And therefore, though they are sick, yet it is just *like* a sickness, and *not* a genuine illness—all things rightly weighed.

When an unskilled eye looks upon the threshing of the corn, he says, 'Why do they spoil the corn?' But those that know better say, 'The flail does not hurt the corn. If the cart wheel should run over it, it would be spoiled indeed, but the flail does not hurt it.' Now there is no affliction or suffering that a godly man meets with which is not God's flail. And if you look at Isaiah 28 you shall find the Lord promises through a picture that his cartwheel will not pass over those that are weak. 'Dill is not threshed with a threshing sledge, nor is a cart wheel rolled over cumin; but dill is beaten out with a stick, and cumin with a rod' (Isa. 28:27). God will always proportion his rod to our strength. 'But, though my affliction is not greater than I can bear, yet if it lies too long upon me,' some might say, 'I shall never be able to bear it.' No, says the Lord in verse 28: When bread is made, the grain is not crushed or threshed forever. But what does this mean for us? It is a parable for verse 26 says: 'For he [speaking of the ploughman] is rightly instructed; his God teaches him.' And if the ploughman has this discretion, how much more shall the Lord himself. For verse 29 says, 'This also comes from the LORD of hosts; he is wonderful in counsel and excellent in wisdom.' 'I am God's corn,' said the martyr, 'I must therefore pass under the flail, through the fan, under the millstone, into the oven before I can be bread for him.' And if our chaff is severed from our graces by this flail, have we any reason to be discouraged because we are thus afflicted?

The truth is the day of affliction and tribulation is a godly man's day of judgment. And it is his *only* judgment day—he shall never be judged again and will not be condemned at the day of judgment. 'But when we are judged by the Lord, we are disciplined so that we may not be condemned along with the world' (1 Cor. 11:32). And when the godly man has a day of affliction he may say, 'Now is my judgment day, and I shall never be judged again.' Why therefore should he be discouraged, whatever his afflictions be?

2. Our Afflictions Come From Divine Love

Second, we will not be discouraged if we consider where the afflictions come from. If all the sufferings of God's people come from divine love, the love of God in Christ to them, then have they no reason to be discouraged, though they are much afflicted. Every rod is a rod of rosemary to them, fruits of their Father's love. And if you look at Hebrews 12 you shall find this proved and applied. It is proved in verse 6, 'For the Lord disciplines the one he loves, and chastises every son whom he receives.' He illustrates this with a picture. Suppose a man has two sons, one illegitimate and the other legitimate. He will give education and correction to the legitimate son, and neglect the illegitimate son. And the Apostle says in verse 8: 'If you are left without discipline… then you are illegitimate children and not sons.' What then? Verse 12 says, 'Therefore, lift up your drooping hands and strengthen your weak knees.' The Apostle says that if all the sufferings and afflictions and chastisements of the saints proceed from love, then they have no reason to hang their heads. And so it is that all their sufferings come from love and there is no reason to be discouraged.

3. Our Afflictions Come With the Grace, Light and Presence of God

Thirdly, consider what comes with the afflictions of the saints. What comes is much supporting grace, so much light, so much of God's presence and fellowship and communion with Christ in all his sufferings.

1. Afflictions Come With Supporting Grace

There is much supporting grace: 'Your rod and your staff, they comfort me' (Psa. 23:4). God never lays a rod upon his children's backs without first putting a staff into their hands to bear it. And the staff is as big as the rod. It does not matter what your afflictions are, great or small, it is all the same: you shall be upheld. And upholding mercy is sometimes better than a mercy your afflictions have removed.

2. Afflictions Reveal Our Sin and God's Grace In Our Lives

But the Lord not only upholds his people under sufferings, but he gives much light with them. The school of the cross is the school of light. Affliction is our free-school where God teaches his children and shows them how to write, both their sins and their graces.

God reveals ours sins through affliction. As long as leaves are on the trees and bushes, you cannot see the birds' nests. But in the winter when all the leaves are off, then you can see them plainly. And as long as men are in prosperity, and have their leaves on, they do not see what nests of sins and lusts are in their hearts and lives. But when all their leaves are off in the day of their afflictions, then they see them and say, 'I didn't realize I had such nests of sins and lusts in my soul and life.' Job 36:7-8 says, 'He does not withdraw his eyes from the righteous … And if they are bound in chains and caught in the chords of affliction, then he declares to them his work and their transgressions, that they are behaving arrogantly.' Moreover, afflictions not only show them their sins, but they are God's plaster by which he heals them. 'Before I was afflicted I went astray', says David (Psa. 119:67). And Job 36:10 says, 'He opens their ears to instruction and commands that they return from iniquity.'

God reveals the fruit of his grace in our lives through affliction. And these afflictions and sufferings of the saints not only uncover and heal their sins, but they make them exercise grace. 'In their distress,' says God in Hosea 5:15, they will 'earnestly seek me.' Indeed, they not only rely on his grace, but discover *more* of his grace, which possibly they never took notice of before. …

3. Afflictions Come With God's Presence

And when is God more present with his people than when they are most afflicted? God is behind our affliction. It was under affliction that heaven opened to Stephen (Acts 7:54-56). Afflictions are often the rusty lock which opens the door into the chamber of God's presence. When was Christ with the three children, but in the very fiery furnace

(Dan. 3)? And you have a standing promise for it: 'When you pass through the waters, I will be with you; and through the rivers, they shall not overwhelm you' (Isa. 43:2). And the Apostle says that 'If you are insulted for the name of Christ, you are blessed, because the Spirit of glory and of God rests upon you' (1 Pet. 4:14). Indeed, as they have most of God when they are most afflicted, so in time of their sufferings they have the most communion and fellowship with Jesus Christ in his sufferings. Therefore the Apostle says in 1 Peter 4:13, 'But rejoice insofar as you share Christ's sufferings, that you may also rejoice and be glad when his glory is revealed.' The word 'participate' is the same that is used in 1 John 1:3, 'Indeed our fellowship is with the Father'. And the same word is used in 1 Corinthians 10:16 concerning the Lord's Supper, 'The cup of blessing that we bless, is it not a participation in the blood of Christ?' You will all grant that you have communion with Christ at the Lord's Supper. But the same word being used here shows that you have communion with Christ in his sufferings also, especially when you suffer for him. And the greater your sufferings are, the more fellowship and communion you have with Christ in his sufferings.

Now then, if all this is true, that a Christian has supporting and upholding grace, much light, that his sin is uncovered and healed, his grace is exercised and manifested, that God's presence is enjoyed, and that he participates in the sufferings of Christ, in and by his afflictions, what reason has he to be discouraged, although he be much afflicted? But so it is that a Christian never has more experience of God's upholding, sustaining grace, his sin is never more uncovered, and healed, his grace is never more exercised and manifested, God is never more present with him, than when he is most afflicted. And he never participates more in Christ's sufferings than in and by his own sufferings. Surely therefore, he has no reason for his discouragements, whatever his afflictions are.

4. Our Afflictions Lead to Glory

Fourthly, consider the fruit, benefit, end and outcome of your afflictions. They bring forth the quiet fruits of righteousness and triumph over Satan. Poor Job may say, 'Satan, you said I did not serve God for nothing, but your claim has been contradicted.' Indeed, 'For this light momentary affliction is preparing for us an eternal weight of glory beyond all comparison' (2 Cor. 4:17). And if you look at Philippians 2:12, where we are commanded to work out our salvation with fear and trembling, you find the word 'work' is the same word as the word translated 'achieving' to describe our afflictions. Our afflictions are at work to produce for us an eternal glory. Now if all my afflictions bring me the quiet fruit of righteousness, make me triumph over Satan, and work out an exceeding weight of glory, have I any reason to be discouraged, although I am much afflicted? Thus it is with all the saints and people of God. Though their sufferings may seem to be grievous for the present, yet they bring forth the quiet fruits of righteousness. By them the saints triumph over Satan and these sufferings work out an exceeding weight of glory. Surely therefore, a godly, gracious man has no reason to be discouraged, whatever his afflictions are.

Further Reading

- William Bridge, *A Lifting Up for the Downcast* (Edinburgh: Banner of Truth, 2009).

- *The Works of William Bridge,* 5 vols. (Ligonier, PA: Soli Deo Gloria Publications, 1990).

5

JEREMIAH BURROUGHS
on Contentment

IN 1617, King James I (of the King James Bible) issued a decree called 'the Book of Sports' specifically permitting dancing, archery and other sports on the Lord's Day. It was intended to resolve a dispute between Puritans and the gentry in Lancashire. But a year later the king required it to be read from pulpits across the nation. At the time Jeremiah Burroughs (1600-1646) was the assistant of Edmund Calamy in Suffolk and for many years both men refused to read it out in their churches. In 1631 Burroughs moved to a church in Norfolk, but eventually his defiance to the king caught up with him and he was forced from his post. So from 1638 to 1640 Burroughs taught in a church of English Independents in Rotterdam in the Netherlands. Burroughs served there alongside William Bridge, the author of *A Lifting Up for the Downcast*. And perhaps it is significant that both these exiles wrote on how we can find contentment in the midst of adversity—they were speaking from their own experience.

Burroughs returned to England during the Commonwealth and served two churches in Stepney and Cripplegate in London. He would preach at 7am (so people could attend before work) and become known as 'the morning star of Stepney'.

Burroughs was also a member of the Westminster Assembly. He was one of a small but highly gifted and vocal group of

Independent Pastors. Since they favoured the self-government of congregations, they caused problems for the Presbyterian majority. But Burroughs worked hard to promote unity among gospel-minded church leaders. A generation later Richard Baxter would say, 'If all the Episcopalians had been like Archbishop Ussher, all the Presbyterians like Stephen Marshall, and all the Independents like Jeremiah Burroughs, the breaches of the church would soon have been healed.' In 1646 Burroughs fell from his horse and died as a result. This sad accident was of course in God's purposes, and although he died in his prime, Burroughs' works are read across the world today, teaching Christians how to live—and to suffer—for Christ.

In *The Rare Jewel of Christian Contentment*, first published in 1648, two years after Burroughs' death, Burroughs starts with the text, 'I have learned, in whatsoever state I am, therewith to be content.' (Phil. 4:11) His aim is to explain what it means to learn to be content. 'To be skilled in the mystery of Christian contentment,' he says, 'is the duty, glory and excellence of a Christian.' Burroughs recognizes that there's a place for 'making in an orderly manner our moan and complaint to God, and to our friends.' He's not asking us to pretend that bad things are not bad or that everything is OK when it's not. Nor does contentment mean we never try to change our situation or end our suffering. But contentment is the antidote to murmuring, fretting, instability, distraction and discouragement. Nor is this simply an outward demeanour: 'A shoe may be smooth and neat outside, while inside it pinches the flesh. Outwardly there may be great calmness and stillness, yet within amazing confusion, bitterness, disturbance and vexation.'[1]

Burroughs defines contentment as 'that sweet, inward, quiet, gracious frame of spirit, which freely submits to and

---

[1] Jeremiah Burroughs, *The Rare Jewel of Christian Contentment*, (Edinburgh: Banner of Truth, 2013), pp. 19-21.

delights in God's wise and fatherly disposal in every condition.[2] Notice that Christian contentment is God-ward in its orientation. It's not just about being happy. It's welcoming our circumstances as God's gracious providence arranged for our good—'taking pleasure in God's disposal'.[3]

A person grows in contentment 'not so much by adding more to his condition; but rather by subtracting from his desires, so as to make his desires and his circumstances even and equal.[4] It's easy to think that if we just get this role or gadget or holiday or home then we would be content. But, says Burroughs, that's a fool's errand. The real secret is to redirect our desires to what we already have in Christ. In the end it is only God who truly satisfies: 'A soul that is capable of God can be filled with nothing else but God; nothing but God can fill a soul that is capable of God.'[5] The flesh thinks, 'I must have my wants made up or else it is impossible that I should be content.' But a gracious hearts says, 'What is the duty of the circumstances God has put me into?' In other words, we turn from looking inwards at our desires and instead look outward in love to pursue the glory of God and the needs of our neighbour. 'A gracious heart is contented by the melting of his will and desires into God's will and desires.'[6]

Things to Look Out For

Notice how Burroughs invites us to look at all the things we enjoy in everyday life as gifts from God and therefore signs of his love. This was a common feature of the Puritan vision. Believing in God's providence, they assumed God's involvement in everything that happened to them, good and bad. So they sought to interpret their lives in the light of God's word.

[2] Burroughs, *Rare Jewel*, p. 19.
[3] *Ibid.*, p. 33.
[4] *Ibid.*, p. 45.
[5] *Ibid.*, p. 43.
[6] *Ibid.*, p. 53.

This is important when Burroughs goes on to reflect on our hardship. We're to let God's word shape how we view our lives and our relationship with God—not our circumstances and not comparisons with other people.

�֎

The Rare Jewel of Christian Contentment

From Chapter 3—The Mystery of Contentment[7]

A gracious heart gets contentment in a mysterious way, a way that the world is not acquainted with …

A Christian Lives upon the Dew of God's Blessing

A Christian can get food that the world does not know about for he is fed in a secret way by the dew of the blessing of God. A poor man or woman who has but a little *with God's grace* lives a more contented life than his rich neighbour who has a great income. We often find that Christians, though they have but little, yet they have a secret blessing of God with it, which they cannot express to anyone else. If you were to come to them and say: 'How is it that you live as happily as you do?', they cannot tell you what they have. But they find there is a sweetness in what they do enjoy, and they know by experience that they never had such sweetness in former times. Even though they had a greater abundance in former times than they have now, yet they know they never had such sweetness. But how this comes about they cannot tell.

We may mention some considerations, in what godly men enjoy, which make their condition sweet. For example, take these four or five considerations with which a godly man finds contentment in what he has, though it is ever so little.

---

[7] Burroughs, *Rare Jewel*, pp. 56-60.

1. Our 'Little' Is a Token of God's Love

In what he has, he has the love of God to him. If a king were to send a piece of meat from his own table, it would be a great deal more pleasant to a courtier than if he had twenty dishes as an ordinary allowance. If the king sends even a little thing and says, 'Go and carry it to that man as a token of my love'— oh, how delightful would that be to him! When your husbands are at sea and send you a token of their love, it is worth more than forty times what you already have in your houses. Every good thing the people of God enjoy, they enjoy in God's love, as a token of God's love, and coming from God's eternal love to them. And this is surely very sweet to them.

2. Our 'Little' is God's Means of Our Sanctification

What Christians have is sanctified to them for good. Other men have what they enjoy in the way of common providence, but the saints have it in a special way. Others have what they have and no more: meat, and drink, and houses, and clothes, and money, and that is all. But a gracious heart finds contentment in this:

> I have it, and I have a sanctified use of it too. I find God goes along with what I have to draw my heart nearer to him, and sanctify my heart to him. If I find my heart drawn nearer to God by what I enjoy, that is much more than if I have it without the sanctifying of my heart by it.

There is a secret dew that goes along with it: the dew of God's love in it, and the dew of sanctification.

3. Our 'Little' is God's Gift Given Without Payment

A gracious heart has what he has free of cost. He is not likely to be called to pay for it. The difference between what a godly man has and a wicked man, is this: a godly man is like a child in an inn. An inn-keeper has his child in the house, and provides his diet, and lodging, and what is needful for him. Now a stranger comes, and he has dinner and supper provided, and lodging. But the stranger must pay for everything. It may be that the child's fare is more humble than the fare of the stranger. The stranger has boiled and roast and baked food, but he must pay for it. There must come a reckoning for it. In the same way, many of God's people have only humble fare, but God as a Father provides it and it is free of cost. They need not pay for what they have. It is paid for already. But the wicked—in all their pomp, and pride, and finery—have what they ask for, but there must come a reckoning for everything. They must pay for all at the conclusion. And is it not better to have a little free of cost than to have to pay for everything? Grace shows a man that what he has, he has free of cost, from God as from a Father, and therefore it must be very sweet.

4. Our 'Little' Is Now Our Right Purchased By Christ

A godly man may very well be content, though he has only a little, for what he does have he has by right of Jesus Christ, by the purchase of Jesus Christ. He has a right to it, a different kind of right to that which a wicked man can have to what he has. Wicked men have certain outward things. I do not say they are usurpers of what they have. They have a right to it, and that before God. But how? It is a right by mere donation. That is, God by his free bounty gives it to them. But the right that the saints have is a right of purchase. It is paid for and it is their own. And they may in a holy manner and holy way claim whatever they need.

We cannot express the difference between the right of a holy man and the right of the wicked more fully than by the following simile. A criminal is condemned to die, and yet by favour he has his supper provided overnight. Now, though the criminal has forfeited all his right to all things, to every bit of bread, yet if he is given his supper he does not steal it. This is true, though he has forfeited all rights by his fault, and after he has once been condemned he has no right to anything. So it is with the wicked. They have forfeited all their right to the comforts of this world. They are condemned by God as criminals and are going to execution. But if God in his bounty gives them something to preserve them here in the world, they cannot be said to be thieves or robbers. But if a man is given such a supper overnight before his execution, is it like the supper that he was used to having in his own house, when he ate his own bread, and had his wife and children about him? Oh, a dish of green herbs at home would be a great deal better than any dainties in such a supper as that.

But a child of God has not a right merely by donation. What he has is his own through the purchase of Christ. Every bit of bread you eat, if you are a godly man or woman, Jesus Christ has bought for you. You go to market and buy your meat and drink with your money, but know that before you buy it or pay money, Christ has bought it at the hand of God the Father with his blood. You have it at the hands of men for money, but Christ has bought it at the hand of his Father by his blood. Certainly it is a great deal better and sweeter now, though it is but a little.

5. Our 'Little' Is the First Instalment of Eternal Glory

There is another thing that shows the sweetness that is in the little that the saints have, by which they come to have contentment, whereas others cannot. It is this. Every little that they have is but as an earnest penny—a first instalment which guarantees that the rest is to follow. It is an earnest of all the glory that is reserved for them. It is given to them by God as the forerunner of those eternal mercies that the Lord intends for them.

Now if a man has but twelve pence given to him as an earnest for some great possession that he must have, is that not better than if he had forty pounds given to him otherwise? So every comfort that the saints have in this world is an earnest to them of those eternal mercies that the Lord has provided for them. Every affliction that the wicked have here is but the beginning of sorrows, and forerunner of those eternal sorrows that they are likely to have hereafter in hell. In the same way, every comfort you have is a forerunner of those eternal mercies you shall have with God in heaven. Not only are the consolations of God's Spirit the forerunners of those eternal comforts you shall have in heaven, but when you sit at your table, and rejoice with your wife and children and friends, you may look upon every one of those as a forerunner, the very earnest of eternal life to you.

Now if this is so, it is no marvel that a Christian is contented. But this is a mystery to the wicked. I have what I have from the love of God, and I have it sanctified to me by God, and I have it free of cost from God by the purchase of the blood of Jesus Christ, and I have it as a forerunner of those eternal mercies that are reserved for me. And in all this my soul rejoices. There is a secret dew of God's goodness and blessing upon him in his estate that others have not. By all this you may see the meaning of that Scripture, 'Better is a little with righteousness than great revenues with injustice' (Prov. 16:8). A man who has but a little, yet if he has it with righteousness, it is better than a great deal without right. Indeed, it is better than the great revenues of the wicked. So the mystery of Christian contentment includes this truth: that a Christian lives on the dew of God's blessing in all the good things that he enjoys.

From Chapter 13—How to Attain Contentment[8]

Choose to Interpret God's Ways As Good

I urge you to observe this, even if you forget many of my other points: *Make a good interpretation of God's ways towards you.* If any good interpretation can be made of God's ways towards you, make it. You would not like it if you had a friend who always makes bad interpretations of your ways towards him. You would take that badly. If you should converse with people with whom you cannot speak a word without them readily interpreting it badly and taking it the wrong way, you would think their company very tedious. It is very tedious to the Spirit of God when we make such bad interpretations of his ways towards us.

When God deals with us otherwise than we would have him do, if one sense worse than another can be put upon it, we should be sure to make a good interpretation of it. Thus, when an affliction befalls you, many good senses may be made of God's works towards you. You should think thus:

- It may be that God intends only to try me by this.

- It may be that God saw my heart was too set on the creature and so he intends to show me what is in my heart.

- It may be that God saw that, if my wealth continued, I should fall into sin—that the better my outward position were the worse my soul would be.

- It may be that God intended only to exercise some grace.

- It may be that God intends to prepare me for some great work which he has for me.

[8] Burroughs, *Rare Jewel*, pp. 223-227.

Thus is the way you should reason.

But we, on the contrary, make bad interpretations of God's dealings with us in this kind of way. We say, 'God does not mean this. Surely the Lord means by this to manifest his wrath and displeasure against me, and this is but a further-ance of further evils that he intends toward me!' This is what the Israelites did in the wilderness: 'God has brought us here to slay us.' This is the worst interpretation that you can possi-bly make of God's ways. Oh, why will you make these worst interpretations when there may be better interpretations? In 1 Corinthians 13:5, when the Scripture speaks of love, it says, Love 'thinks no evil' (NKJV). Love is of that nature that if ten interpretations may be made of a thing, nine of them bad and one good, love will take that which is good and leave the other nine. And so, though ten interpretations might be presented to you concerning God's way towards you, and if but one is good and nine bad, you should take that one which is good, and leave the other nine.

I urge you to consider that God does not deal with you as you deal with him. If God were to make the worst interpre-tation of all your ways towards him, as you do of his ways towards you, it would be very ill with you. God is pleased to manifest his love to us by making the best interpretations of what we do. And therefore God attributes a meaning to the action of his people that one would think could hardly be. For example, God is pleased to call those perfect who have any uprightness of heart in them. He accounts them perfect. 'Be perfect as your heavenly Father is perfect.' Uprightness in God's sense is perfection. Now, alas, when we look into our own hearts we can scarce see any good at all there, and yet God is pleased to make such an interpretation as to say, 'It is perfect'. When we look into our own hearts, we can see nothing but uncleanness. Yet God calls you his *saints*. He calls the lowest Christian who has the least grace under the greatest corruption his *saint*. You say we cannot be saints here. But yet in God's esteem we are saints. You know the usual title the Holy Spirit gives, in several of the New Testament Epistles, to those who had any grace, any uprightness, is, To the *saints* in such a place. You see what an interpretation God puts upon them: they are saints to him. And so I might name many other ways in which God makes the best interpretation of things. If there is an abundance of evil and a little good, God rather passes by the evil and takes notice of the good.

I have sometimes made use of a very notable place in 1 Peter concerning Sarah. Sarah spoke to her husband in Genesis 18:12 and there she called her husband 'lord'. It was only one good word in a bad, unbelieving speech. And yet when the Apostle mentions that speech in 1 Peter 3:6, the Holy Spirit leaves all the bad and commends her for calling her husband 'lord', for putting a reverent title upon her husband. This is how graciously God deals with us! If there is but one good word among a great many ill, what an interpretation God makes! So should we do. If there is only one good interpretation that we can make of a thing we should rather make use of the good one than the bad. Oh, my brethren (I would I could now speak only to such as are godly), retain good thoughts of God. Take heed of judging God to be a hard master. Make good interpretations of his ways. And this will be a special means to help you to contentment in all one's course.

Don't Let Other People and Their Possessions Define Your Contentment

Do not look at the luxuries of other men to define what you feel you yourselves need. For the reason for our discontentment many times comes from the luxuries of other men rather than what we ourselves actually lack. We think poverty to be such a great evil. Why? Because this is how other people think of it. It's not because we actually feel a sense of lack—unless we're in extreme poverty.

I will give you a clear demonstration that almost all the discontent in the world comes from the luxuries of others rather than from the evil that is on people themselves. You may think your wealth to be small and you are therefore discontented and it is a grievous affliction to you. But if all men in the world were poorer than you then you would not be discontented. Then you would rejoice in your estates, even though you had not a penny more than you have now. Suppose you earn just twelve pence a day. You will say, 'This is but a poor thing to maintain a family'. But suppose there were no man in the world that had more than this. Indeed, suppose all other men but you had somewhat less wages than this. Then you would think your condition pretty good. But in fact you would have no more then than you have now. Therefore it is clear from this that it is rather the luxuries of other men, rather than what you actually feel, that makes you think your condition is so grievous. For if all the men in the world looked upon you as happy, more happy than themselves, then you would be contented.

Oh, do not let your happiness depend upon the luxuries of other men. There is a saying of Chrysostom, the early church father: 'Let us not make the people in this case to be our lords. Just as we must not make men lords of our faith, so let us not make them the lords of our comforts.' That is, our comfort should not depend more upon their imaginations than upon what we feel in ourselves. It may be that others think you to be in an afflicted condition. But I thank God for myself that I do not know this. Were it not for the disgrace, disregard and slightings of other men, my condition would not be so bad to me as it is now. This is what makes my condition afflictive.

Don't Make Your Present Comforts and Possessions the Focus of Your Joy

Be not inordinately taken up with the comforts of this world when you have them. When you have them, do not take too much satisfaction in them. It is a certain rule: however inordinate any man or woman is in sorrow when a comfort is taken from them, so were they immoderate in their rejoicing in the comfort when they had it. For instance, suppose God takes away a child and you are inordinately sorrowful, beyond what God allows in a natural or Christian way. Now, though I never knew before how your heart was towards the child, yet when I see this, I see your heart. Even though you are a mere stranger to me, I may without breach of charity conclude that your heart was immoderately set upon your child, or husband, or upon any other comfort that I see you grieving for when God has taken it away.

Suppose you hear ill tidings about your estates, and your hearts are dejected immoderately, and you are in a discontented mood because of such and such a cross. Then it is certain that your hearts were immoderately set upon the world. So, likewise, with your reputation. If you hear others report this or that ill of you, and your hearts are dejected because you think you suffer in your name, your hearts were inordinately set upon your name and reputation. Now, therefore, the way for you not to be immoderate in your sorrow for afflictions is not to be immoderate in your love and delights when you have prosperity.

My brethren, to conclude this point, if I were to tell you that I could show you a way never to be in want of anything, then no doubt we would have many people flocking to such a sermon. Many people would want to hear a man show people how they might never be in want any more. But what I have been preaching to you now comes to the same thing. It amounts to the same thing and produces the same effect.

Is it not almost the same: never to be in want and never to be without contentment? That man or woman who is never without a contented spirit can truly be said never to want much. Oh, the Word holds forth a way full of comfort and peace to the people of God, even in this world. You may live happy lives in the midst of all the storms and tempests in the world. There is an ark that you may come into, and no-one in the world may live such comfortable, cheerful and contented lives as the saints of God.

Further Reading

- Jeremiah Burroughs, *The Rare Jewel of Christian Content-ment* (Edinburgh: Banner of Truth, 2013).

- A number of other works by Burroughs have been reprinted by Soli Deo Gloria Publications, which is now part of Reformation Heritage Books.

6

ANNE BRADSTREET
on Loss

But when thou northward to me shalt return,
I wish my Sun may never set, but burn
within the Cancer of my glowing breast,
the welcome house of him, my dearest guest,
where ever, ever stay, and go not thence,
till nature's sad decree shall call thee hence.
Flesh of thy flesh, bone of thy bone,
I here, thou there, yet both but one.

SO writes the Puritan poet Anne Bradstreet (1612–1672).
It is not perhaps the type of poetry one associates with
the Puritans. They have sadly gained the reputation of being
against pleasure, especially sexual pleasure. Their name
has become a colloquial term for being anti-fun. Occasion-
ally this reputation is deserved, but more often the Puritans
were patrons of the arts with a zest for life. We also need to
remember that what today seem to us to be innocent pleasures (like going to the theatre) were not so innocent in the
seventeenth century (when theatres were bawdy places, their
pleasures often consciously set against the gospel, and also
associated with prostitution). The Puritans did have a strong
awareness of the importance of the next life (and Bradstreet's

poetry exemplifies this). But they also embraced this world as a gift from God. Yes, they took life seriously, but that included work, family, leisure, art (especially literature) and, yes, sex. Bradstreet was one of the first poets in the English language to publish poems celebrating marital love.

Anne Bradstreet was born in 1612, probably in Northampton. In 1628, aged sixteen, she married Simon Bradstreet, the son of a Puritan vicar. Within two years they had sailed to America with Anne's parents. King Charles I and Archbishop William Laud were rolling back Reformation changes in England, moving the country in a more Catholic direction. The Bradstreets were part of an exodus to America during this period that had been kick-started by the Pilgrim Fathers on the *Mayflower* ten years before.

Anne was seventeen when she stepped onto the shores of America. It had been settled by Europeans for not much more than a hundred years and conditions were still harsh. Several people died during the Atlantic crossing and during the first winter, two hundred of the one thousand settlers in the area died of starvation. That winter was known as 'the starving time'. It was a world of promise and freedom with the hope of a new beginning for those early Puritans, but it was also a precarious world.

Initially Anne was unhappy and it was a couple of years before she 'resigned' herself to her new life. 'Resignation' is a common concept in Puritan spirituality. It means finding contentment in the life God has given us. Anne herself eventually found this 'resignation' as a result of a period of sickness. It was common for Puritans to see adversities as designed by God to sanctify us. In 'Deliverance from Another Sore Fit' Anne thanks God 'even for His mercies in His rod, where pity most of all I see'.

What to Look Out For

Writing poetry was considered a male occupation and some of Anne's poems were published under a male pseudonym. At times Anne was prepared to challenge the social order. Her longest poem, styled as a dialogue between New England (the American colonies) and Old England, is a political poem, lamenting the oppression of Puritan ministry and the decline of English liberties. Yet in other ways she is conservative. 'Her Mother's Epitaph' reflects the Puritan ideal of a godly woman, while 'Her Father's Epitaph' does the same for a man. There was no confusion of gender roles in her worldview. So, while the Puritans pushed the social boundaries, they did so within the boundaries of Scripture. They were committed to the rule of Scriptures. Whether that made them radicals or conservatives simply depended on the political currents going on around them.

For much of the time today we can avoid the reality of death. People, for example, rarely die at home and we rarely see dead bodies. But Anne wrote with a strong sense of the immanence of death. Childbirth was so precarious that in the poem 'Before the Birth of One of Her Children' Anne bids farewell to the world. The transitory nature of life and the glorious hope that awaits those who trust in Christ are perhaps the dominant themes of her poetry. For the Puritans life is to be used to prepare for death and we should hold the glories of this world lightly. Death undermines the achievements of this life. Only identity in Christ lasts into eternity. In 'The Flesh and the Spirit' she imagines an argument between the flesh and the Spirit along the lines described in Galatians 5:16-17. But the focus is on the competing value of earthly treasure and heavenly treasure (Matt. 6:20-24). Alluding to Revelation 2:17, she writes in a poem entitled 'Contemplations':

O Time, the fatal wrack of mortal things,
that draws oblivious curtains over kings,
their sumptuous monuments, men know them not,
their names without a record are forgot,
Their parts, their ports, their pomp's all laid in th'dust;
nor wit, nor gold, nor buildings scape time's rust.
But he whose name is grav'd in the white stone
shall last and shine when all of these are gone.

This was a particular issue for Anne for she and her family moved to yet more remote areas, facing the threat of attack from native Americans. Unusually all of eight of her children survived infancy, but not her grandchildren. In 1665 one grandchild, Elizabeth, died. In 1666 fire destroyed their home. In 1668 another grandchild, also named Anne, died. Then in 1669 a grandson, Simon, died as well as one of her daughters-in-law. On the death of the granddaughter named after her, Anne wrote:

With troubled heart and trembling hand I write,
The heavens have chang'd to sorrow my delight.
How oft with disappointment have I met,
Farewell dear child, thou ne're shall come to me,
but yet a while, and I shall go to thee.
Mean time my throbbing heart's chear'd up with this:
thou with thy Saviour art in endless bliss.

In a poem, written when fire consumed their home, Anne laments all she has lost. She recalls her distress as the fire took hold. There is a real sense of loss expressed in this poem as she recounts the ruined possessions that she loved. But then she speaks to herself, reminding herself of the truth, calling on her heart to look to things above.

To reflect the metre of Bradstreet's poems you normally need to pronounce the suffix '-ed' as a separate syllable—'blessèd' rather than 'blessed' (unless the 'e' is replaced by an apostrophe).

✳

Selected Poems

A Letter to Her Husband Absent upon Public Employment

My head, my heart, mine eyes, my life, nay more,
my joy, my magazine[1] of earthly store,
if two be one, as surely thou and I,
how stayest thou there, whilst I at Ipswich lie?
So many steps, head from the heart to sever,
if but a neck, soon should we be together.
I, like the earth this season, mourn in black,
my Sun is gone so far in's Zodiac,
whom whilst I 'joy'd, nor storms, nor frost I felt,
his warmth such frigid colds did cause to melt.
My chilled limbs now numbed lie forlorn;
return; return, sweet Sol[2], from Capricorn.
In this dead time, alas, what can I more
than view those fruits which through thy heart I
 bore?
Which sweet contentment yield me for a space,
true living pictures of their father's face.
O strange effect! Now thou art southward gone,
I weary grow, the tedious day so long.
But when thou northward to me shalt return,
I wish my Sun may never set, but burn
within the Cancer[3] of my glowing breast,
the welcome house of him my dearest guest.
Where ever, ever stay, and go not thence,

[1] magazine = store.   [2] sol = sun.   [3] Cancer = the constellation.

till nature's sad decree shall call thee hence.
Flesh of thy flesh, bone of thy bone,
I here, thou there, yet both but one.

To My Dear and Loving Husband

If ever two were one, then surely we.
If ever man were lov'd by wife, then thee.
If ever wife was happy in a man,
compare with me, ye women, if you can.
I prize thy love more than whole mines of gold,
or all the riches that the east doth hold.
My love is such that rivers cannot quench,
nor ought but love from thee give recompense.
Thy love is such I can no way repay.
The heavens reward thee manifold, I pray.
Then while we live, in love let's so persevere
that when we live no more, we may live ever.

Mother's Epitaph

An Epitaph on my dear and ever honoured Mother, Mrs Dorothy
Dudley, who deceased, December 27, 1643, aged 61.

Here lies
a worthy matron of unspotted life,
a loving mother and obedient wife,
a friendly neighbour, pitiful to poor,
whom oft she fed, and clothed with her store;
to servants wisely aweful, but yet kind,
and as they did, so they reward did find:
A true instructor of her family,
the which she ordered with dexterity.
The public meetings[1] ever did frequent,
and in her closet constant hours she spent.[2]

---

[1] meetings of the church.   [2] see Matt. 6:6 KJV.

Religious in all her words and ways,
preparing still for death, till end of days.
Of all her children, children lived to see,
then dying, left a blessed memory.

Father's Epitaph

To the memory of my dear and ever honoured Father, Thomas
Dudley Esq, who deceased, July 31, 1653, aged 77.

Within this tomb a patriot lies
that was both pious, just and wise,
to truth a shield, to right a wall,
to sectaries[1] a whip and maul,
a magazine[2] of history,
a prizer of good company,
in manners pleasant and severe,
the good him loved, the bad did fear,
and when his time with years was spent
if some rejoiced, more did lament.

The Flesh and the Spirit

In secret place where once I stood
close by the Banks of Lacrim[3] flood,
I heard two sisters reason on
things that are past and things to come.
One Flesh was call'd, who had her eye
on worldly wealth and vanity.
The other Spirit, who did rear
her thoughts unto a higher sphere.
'Sister,' quoth Flesh, 'what liv'st thou on?
Nothing but meditation?
Doth contemplation feed thee so
regardlessly to let earth go?

[1] sectaries = sectarians.   [2] magazine = store.   [3] Lacrim = tears.

Can speculation satisfy?
Notion without reality?
Dost dream of things beyond the moon
and dost thou hope to dwell there soon?
Hast treasures there laid up in store
that all in th' world thou count'st but poor?
Art fancy-sick or turn'd a sot[1]
to catch at shadows which are not?
Come, come, I'll show unto thy sense,
industry hath its recompense.
What canst desire, but thou mayest see
true substance in variety?
Dost *honour* like? Acquire the same,
as some to their immortal fame;
and trophies to thy name erect
which wearing time shall ne'er deject.
For *riches* dost thou long full sore?
Behold enough of precious store.
Earth hath more silver, pearls and gold
than eyes can see, or hands can hold.
Affects thou *pleasure*? Take thy fill,
earth hath enough of what you will.
Then let not go what thou mayest find
for things unknown, only in mind.'

Spirit: 'Be still, thou unregenerate part,
disturb no more my settled heart.
For I have vow'd (and so will do)
thee as a foe still to pursue.
And combat with thee will and must,
until I see thee laid in th' dust.
Sisters we are, yea twins we be,

[1] sot = drunkard.   [2] shews = shows.

yet deadly feud 'twixt thee and me.
For from one father are we not.
Thou by old Adam wast begot.
But my arise is from above,
whence my dear Father I do love.
Thou speak'st me fair but hat'st me sore.
Thy flatt'ring shews I'll trust no more.
How oft thy slave hast thou me made
when I believ'd what thou hast said.
And never had more cause of woe
than when I did what thou bad'st do.
I'll stop mine ears at these thy charms
and count them for my deadly harms.
Thy sinful pleasures I do hate;
thy riches are to me no bait.
Thine honours do, nor will I love,
for my ambition lies above.
My greatest honour it shall be
when I am victor over thee,
and triumph shall, with laurel head,
when thou my captive shalt be led.
How I do live, thou need'st not scoff,
for I have meat thou know'st not of.[1]
The hidden Manna I do eat;[2]
the word of life, it is my meat.
My thoughts do yield me more content
than can thy hours in pleasure spent.
Nor are they shadows which I catch,
nor fancies vain at which I snatch,
but reach at things that are so high,
beyond thy dull capacity.

[1] see John 4:31-34.   [2] see Revelation 2:17.

Eternal substance I do see
with which enriched I would be.
Mine eye doth pierce the heav'ns, and see
what is invisible to thee.
My garments are not silk nor gold,
nor such like trash which earth doth hold,
but royal robes I shall have on,
more glorious than the glistering Sun.
My crown, not diamonds, pearls and gold,
but such as angels' heads enfold.
The City where I hope to dwell,[1]
there's none on Earth can parallel.
The stately walls both high and strong
are made of precious jasper stone,
The gates of pearl, both rich and clear,
and angels are for porters there.
The streets thereof transparent gold,
such as no eye did e're behold.
A crystal river there doth run
which doth proceed from the Lamb's throne.
Of Life, there are the waters sure,
which shall remain forever pure.
Nor Sun nor Moon they have no need,
for glory doth from God proceed.
No candle there, nor yet torch-light,
for there shall be no darksome night.
From sickness and infirmity
forevermore they shall be free.
Nor withering age shall e're come there,
but beauty shall be bright and clear.
This City pure is not for thee,
for things unclean there shall not be.

[1] see Revelation 21:9-22:5.

If I of heav'n may have my fill;
take thou the world, and all that will.'

Before the Birth of One of Her Children

All things within this fading world hath end;
adversity doth still our joys attend.
No ties so strong, no friends so dear and sweet,
but with death's parting blow is sure to meet.
The sentence past is most irrevocable,
a common thing, yet oh, inevitable.
How soon, my dear, death may my steps attend.
How soon't may be thy lot to lose thy friend.
We both are ignorant, yet love bids me
these farewell lines to recommend to thee,
that when that knot's untied that made us one,
I may seem thine, who in effect am none.
And if I see not half my days that's due,
what nature would, God grant to yours and you.
The many faults that well you know I have,
let be interred in my oblivion's grave.
If any worth or virtue were in me,
let that live freshly in thy memory.
And when thou feel'st no grief, as I no harms,
yet love thy dead, who long lay in thine arms.
And when thy loss shall be repaid with gains,
look to my little babes, my dear remains.
And if thou love thyself, or loved'st me,
these O protect from step-dame's[1] injury.
And if chance to thine eyes shall bring this verse,
with some sad sighs honour my absent hearse;
and kiss this paper for thy love's dear sake,
who with salt tears this last farewell did take.

Upon a Fit of Sickness, 1632

Twice ten years old, not fully told
   since nature gave me breath,
my race is run, my thread spun,
   lo, here is fatal death.
All men must die, and so must I;
   this cannot be revoked.
For Adam's sake, this word God spake
   when he so high provok'd.
Yet live I shall, this life's but small,
   in place of highest bliss,
where I shall have all I can crave,
   no life is like to this.
For what's this life, but care and strife
   since first we came from womb?
Our strength doth waste, our time doth haste,
   and then we go to th' tomb.
O bubble blast, how long can'st last?
   that always art a-breaking,
no sooner blown, but dead and gone,
   ev'n as a word that's speaking.
O whilst I live, this grace me give,
   I doing good may be,
then death's arrest I shall count best,
   because it's thy decree.
Bestow much cost there's nothing lost,
   to make salvation sure.
O great's the gain, though got with pain,
   comes by profession pure.
The race is run, the field is won,
   the victory's mine I see;

---

[1] step-dame = stepmother.

Forever know, thou envious foe,
　　the foil belongs to thee.

Verses upon the Burning of Our House, July 18th, 1666

In silent night when rest I took,
for sorrow near I did not look,
I waken'd was with thund'ring noise
and piteous shrieks of dreadful voice.
That fearful sound of 'fire' and 'fire',
let no man know is my desire.

I, starting up, the light did spy,
and to my God my heart did cry
to strengthen me in my distress
and not to leave me succourless.
Then coming out, behold a space,
the flame consume my dwelling place.

And, when I could no longer look,
I blest his Name that gave and took,[1]
that laid my goods now in the dust.
Yea, so it was, and so 'twas just.
It was his own; it was not mine.
Far be it that I should repine,

He might of all justly bereft
but yet sufficient for us left.
When by the ruins oft I past,
my sorrowing eyes aside did cast,
and here and there the places spy
where oft I sat, and long did lie.

[1] see Job 1:20-21.

Here stood that trunk, and there that chest,
there lay that store I counted best,
My pleasant things in ashes lie,
and them behold no more shall I.
Under the roof no guest shall sit,
nor at thy table eat a bit.

No pleasant talk shall 'ere be told,
nor things recounted done of old.
No candle 'ere shall shine in thee,
nor bridegroom's voice ere heard shall be.
In silence ever shalt thou lie:
Adieu, adieu, all's vanity.

Then straight I 'gin my heart to chide:
And did thy wealth on earth abide?
Didst fix thy hope on mould'ring dust?
The arm of flesh didst make thy trust?
Raise up thy thoughts above the sky
that dunghill mists away may fly.

Thou hast a house on high erect,
fram'd by that mighty Architect,
with glory richly furnished,
stands permanent, though this be fled.
It's purchased and paid for too,
by him who hath enough to do.

A price so vast as is unknown,
yet by his gift is made thine own.
There's wealth enough; I need no more.

¹ pelf = wealth.

Farewell my pelf;[1] farewell my store.
The world no longer let me love,
my hope and treasure lies above.

Further Reading

Most of Anne Bradstreet's poems are available online.

- Anne Bradstreet, *The Works of Anne Bradstreet*, ed. John Harvard Ellis (Abram E. Cutter, 1867).

- Faith Cook, *Anne Bradstreet: Pilgrim and Poet* (Darlington: Evangelical Press, 2010).

- Garry J. Williams, 'Identity and Loss on the Edge of the Word: Anne Bradstreet (1612-72)', in *Silent Witnesses: Lessons on Theology, Life, and the Church from Christians of the Past* (Edinburgh: Banner of Truth, 2013), pp. 127-139.

7

JOHN OWEN
on Communion with God

JOHN Owen (1616–1683) was one of England's greatest theologians, perhaps its greatest. He was born in Oxfordshire and studied in Oxford until forced to leave by Archbishop William Laud's anti-Puritan measures. Owen became a pastor in Essex, at Fordham and then at Coggeshall. During the English Civil War he was a chaplain to Oliver Cromwell and was appointed by Parliament as Dean of Christ Church, Oxford, and then Vice-chancellor of the University. When Charles II came to the throne Owen was again expelled from Oxford University and started a church in his home in Stadhampton, the village in which he grew up. At one point he was offered a senior Bishopric in the Church of England if he would give up his Congregational convictions, but Owen was a man of integrity and refused. For the next twenty or so years he was an acknowledged leader of Nonconformity (churches dissenting from the practices and polity of the Church of England). Owen wrote many books in both English and Latin—theological treatises, commentaries and pastoral works—and his preaching was in high demand.

In *Communion with God,* Owen explores how we can enjoy a living relationship with God. Key, he argues, is to relate to each distinct member of the Trinity. The book then explores how the Father, Son and Spirit each relate to us and how we are to respond.

The section on the Father has been one of the major influences on my life. Without the gospel, says Owen, we think of God as full of wrath against sin. But 'the great discovery of the gospel' is that God is a Father who is 'full of love'. Love is the particular characteristic of the Father (though Owen is also clear that to encounter one member of the Trinity to encounter them all). So Owen invites us to 'leave behind all our wanderings and our other loves to rest in God alone, and to be satisfied and content in him.' In a striking phrase Owen imagines Jesus saying to us, 'Nothing you can do will more trouble and burden God the Father than not believing that he loves you.'[1]

The Father's love is mediated to us by Christ. 'He is the treasury in which the Father places all the riches of his grace, taken from the bottomless mine of his eternal love. And he is the priest into whose hand we put all the offerings that we return unto the Father.' But Owen is also keen to stress that it's not that the work of Christ secures God's love for us - it's the other way round. God's love is the reason for Christ's work of salvation. It all begins with God's love. God's love is eternal and free. Does this mean God loves his people when they are sinning? 'Yes,' says Owen, 'he loves his people, but not their sinning'. The purpose of love to them does not change. But the form it takes may change as he disciplines his people to lead them back to himself. 'But woe, woe would it be to us,' adds Owen, 'if he were ever to change in his love or take away his kindness from us!'[2]

Things to Look Out For

Owen's main point again and again is that believers need to see God as a loving Father, otherwise they will be plagued by

[1] John Owen, *The Works of John Owen*, Vol. 2 (Edinburgh: Banner of Truth, 2009), pp. 19, 26, 21.
[2] *Ibid.*, pp. 27, 31.

insecurity or keep their distance from him. Only when we see God as the loving Father that he is will we delight in him. This is the remedy to so many of our spiritual problems.

Notice, too, the link Owen makes between human obedience and divine love. Obedience without faith is a horrible legalism. And this can sometimes make Christians suspicious of calls to obedience. But Owen sees obedience as the natural response of those who love God and loving God is faith's response to God's love to us.

❄

Communion with God

From Chapter 3—Of the Particular and Distinctive Communion Which the Saints Have with the Father[3]

How We Respond to the Father's Love

Christians often have exceedingly troubled hearts, worrying about what the Father thinks of them. They are persuaded of the Lord Christ and his good-will. The difficulty lies in their acceptance with the Father. What is his heart towards them? 'Show us the Father and it is enough for us' (John 14:8). Now, this concern ought to be far from their minds. For his love ought to be looked on as the fountain from which all other sweetnesses flow.

This is that what see in the Scriptures: *there is love in the person of the Father particularly which is held out to the saints, through which he will and does have communion with them.*

Now, to complete communion with the Father in love, two things are required of believers: (1) *That they receive it of him.* (2) *That they make appropriate responses to him.*

[3] Owen, *Works*, Vol. 2, pp. 21-24.

1. We receive the Father's love by faith

Communion consists in *giving and receiving*. Until the love of the Father is received, we have no communion with him. How, then, is this love of the Father to be received, so that we have fellowship with him? I answer, *By faith*. The receiving of it is the believing of it. God has so fully, so eminently revealed his love, that it may be received by faith. 'You believe in God,' that is, the Father (John 14:1). And what is to be believed in him? His love— for he is 'love' (1 John 4:8).

It is true that the *immediate* act of faith is not upon the Father, but upon the Son. 'I am the way, and the truth, and the life. No one comes to the Father except through me' (John 14:6). Jesus is the merciful high priest over the house of God, by whom we have access to the throne of grace. He is our introduction to the Father. By him we believe in God (1 Pet. 1:21).

But this is what I say: When by and through Christ we have an access to the Father, we then behold his glory as well and then we see the love that he particularly bears towards us. And this is what we put our faith in. We are then, I say, to eye it, to believe it, to receive it, as in Christ. The outcomes and fruits of God's love are made out to us through Christ alone. No light comes to us except through beams of light. Yet through those beams we see the sun which is the fountain of light. Though all our refreshment lies in *streams* of water, yet by them we are led up to the *fountain*. Jesus Christ, in respect of the love of the Father, is but the beam and the stream. In him all our light and our refreshment lies. Yet by him we are led to the fountain, the sun of eternal love itself.

If believers would exercise their faith in this way, they would find it leads to a big *spiritual* improvement in their walk with God. This is what we are aiming for. Many dark and disturbing thoughts are likely to arise in this matter. Few can carry their hearts and minds up to this height by faith so that their souls rest in the love of the Father. They live below it in the troublesome region of hopes and fears, storms and clouds. In the love of God all is serene and quiet. But they do not know how to attain to this level. This is the will of God, that he may always be looked on as benign, kind, tender, loving and unchangeably so. God especially wants to be seen as the Father, the great fountain and spring of all gracious communications and fruits of love. This is that which Christ came to reveal: God as a Father (John 1:18). This is the name which Christ declares to those who are given to him out of the world (John 17:6). And this is that which Jesus effectually leads us, as he is the only way of going to God as a Father (John 14:5-6). That is, the only way to God is to realize he is love.

By seeing his love, God gives us the rest which he promises. For the love of the Father is the only rest of the soul. It is true, as we have said, we do not do this *formally* in the first instant of believing. We believe in God through Christ (1 Pet. 1:21). Faith seeks out rest for the soul. This is presented to it by Christ, the mediator, as its only cause. But it does not remain here, for by Christ it has access to the Father and his love (Eph. 2:18). Faith finds out that he is love with a design, a purpose of love, a good pleasure towards us from eternity—a delight in us, a contentment with us, a good-will towards us in Christ. And so all the causes of anger and opposition have been taken away. In this way the soul, by faith through Christ, and by him, is brought into the bosom of God. It receives a comforting persuasion and spiritual perception and sense of his love. And so there it remains and rests itself. This is the first thing the saints do in their communion with the Father. We will return to how this can be improved in due course.

2. We Respond to the Father's Love with Love

The appropriate *response* which is required also consists in love. God loves that he may be beloved. When he comes to command the return of the love we have received from him, to complete communion with him, he says, 'My son, give me you heart,' your affections, your love (Prov. 23:26). 'Love the Lord your God with all your heart and with all your soul and with all your strength and with all your mind' (Luke 10:27). This is the response that he demands. When the soul sees God, in his dispensation of love, to be love, to be infinitely lovely and loving, and when it rests on and delights in him as such, then has it communion with him in love. This is love, that God loves us first, and then we love him again.

I shall not now go into a description of divine love. Generally, love is an affection of union and nearness in which we are satisfied in the object of our love. Whenever the Father is looked on in any way other than as acting in love towards the soul it breeds in the soul a dread and aversion. This is why sinners fly from God and hide from God in the Scriptures. But when he who is the Father is considered as a father, acting in love towards the soul, then love rises in the soul again. This is, in faith, the basis of all acceptable obedience (Deut. 5:10; Exod. 20:6; Deut. 10:12, 11:1, 13; 13:3).

Thus this whole business stated by the Apostle: 'He chose us in him before the foundation of the world, that we should be holy and without blame before him in love' (Eph. 1:4 NKJV). It begins in the *love of God* and ends in *our love to him*.

From Chapter 4—Inferences of the Doctrine Concerning Communion with the Father in Love[4]

Having thus discovered the nature of that distinctive communion which we have with the Father, it remains for us give some relevant exhortations, directions and observations.

---

[4] Owen, *Works*, Vol. 2, pp. 31-37.

First, it is evident that Christians rarely exercise this duty of holding direct communion with the Father in love. Being unacquainted with our mercies and our privileges is our sin as well as our trouble. We do not listen to the voice of the Spirit which is given to us, 'that we might understand the things freely given us by God' (1 Cor. 2:12). This makes us go heavily when we might rejoice; and to be weak when we might be strong in the Lord. How few of the saints are acquainted in their experience with this privilege of holding direct communion with the Father in love! With what anxious, doubtful thoughts do they look upon him! What fears and what questioning do they have of his good-will and kindness! At the best, many think there is no sweetness at all in him towards us, but what is purchased at the high price of the blood of Jesus. It is true that the blood of Jesus is the only way God's love is communicated to us. But the free fountain and spring of all is in the bosom of the Father. The 'eternal life, which was with the Father and was made manifest to us' (1 John 1:2).

Look on the Father as Love

Let us, then, look on the Father as love. Do not always look not on him as an angry father, but as one who is most kind and tender. Let us look on him by faith as one that has had thoughts of kindness towards us from everlasting. It is a misapprehension of God that makes anyone run from him who has received anything of the breath of God's Spirit in them. 'They that know you will put their trust in you.' Men cannot remain with God in spiritual meditation. God loses the company of souls because they lack this insight into his love. They fix their thoughts only on his terrible majesty, severity and greatness, and so their spirits do not find God dear to them. Would a soul continually look on his everlasting tenderness and compassion, his thoughts of kindness that have been from of old, his present gracious acceptance, it could not bear an hour's absence from him. But now, perhaps, it cannot watch with him one hour. Let, then, this be the saints' first notion of the Father: that he one who is full of eternal, free love towards them. Let their hearts and thoughts be filled with these thoughts, breaking through all discouragements that lie in the way.

To raise their thoughts in this way, let them consider *whose* love it is. It is the love of him who is in himself all sufficient, infinitely satiated with himself and his own glorious excellencies and perfections. He has no need to go forth with his love to others, nor to seek an object of love apart himself. There might he rest with delight and satisfaction for all eternity. He is sufficient unto his own love. He had his Son, also, his eternal Wisdom, to rejoice and delight himself in from all eternity (Prov. 8:30). This might have taken up and satiated the whole delight of the Father. But he chose to love his saints also. And it is therefore such a love, that seeks not only his own satisfaction, but our good also. It is therefore the love of a God and the love of a Father whose natural outgoings are kindness and bounty. Let, I say, the soul frequently look at the love of the Father for considering this conquers and endears every soul.

Receive the Father's Love by Faith

So look on the Father's love so as to receive it. Unless this be added, all is in vain as far to any communion with God is concerned. We do not hold communion with him in anything until it be received by faith. This, then, is that which I would provoke the saints of God to do, namely to believe this love that God has for them. I would have them believe that such is the heart of the Father towards them and accept of his witness of this. We do not experience the sweetness of love until we receive by faith.

Continually, then, remind yourself of God's love to you, of the way he embraces you with eternal, free love. When the

Lord is, by his word, presented as such to you, let your mind know it and assent that it is so; let your will embrace it; and let all your affections be filled with it. Set your whole heart on it. Let your heart be bound with the cords of this love. If the King is held captive by tresses of hair with your love (Song 7:5), should you not be bound in heaven with his?

Respond to the Father's Love with Love

Let the Father's love have its proper fruit and effect upon your heart in the return of love to him again. So shall we walk in the light of God's face, and have holy communion with our Father all the day long. Let us not deal unkindly with him, and slight him in response to his good-will. Let there not be such a heart in us that would deal so unthankfully with our God.

Now, to help us in this duty, and the daily constant practice of it, I shall add one or two considerations that may be important.

1. God delights in us when we receive his love by faith

It is exceeding acceptable to God, even our Father, that we should thus hold communion with him in his love, that he may be received into our souls as one full of love, tenderness and kindness towards us. Flesh and blood is prone to have very hard thoughts of him—to think he is always angry, yes, implacable. We think that it is not for poor creatures to draw close to him. We think that nothing in the world is more desirable than never to come into his presence or see him at work. 'Who among us can dwell with the consuming fire? Who among us can dwell with everlasting burnings?' say the sinners in Zion (Isa. 33:14). And, 'I was afraid of you, because you are a severe man,' says the evil servant in the gospels (Luke 19:21).

Now, there is nothing more grievous to the Lord, nor more part the design of Satan on the soul, than such thoughts as these. Satan claps his hands (if I may so say) when he can fill the soul with such thoughts of God. In this way, Satan has enough, all that he desires. This has been his design and way from the beginning. The first blood shed by a murderer was by this means. Satan led our first parents into hard thoughts of God: 'Has God said so? Has he threatened you with death? He knows well enough eating the forbidden fruit will be better with you.' With this engine he battered and over-threw all mankind in one. And, being mindful of his ancient conquest, he readily uses the same weapons with which he then so successfully contended. Now, it is exceeding griev-ous to the Spirit of God to be so slandered in the hearts of those whom he dearly loves. How he protests this with Zion! 'What wrong did your fathers find in me?' he says (Jer. 2:5). 'Have I been a wilderness to you, or a land of darkness?' Zion said, 'My way is hidden from the LORD; and my right is disre-garded by my God' (Isa. 40:27).

> Can a woman forget her nursing child,
>> that she should have no compassion on the son of her womb?
> Even these may forget,
>> yet I will not forget you.
> Behold, I have engraved you on the palms of my hands;
>> your walls are continually before me (Isa. 49:15-16).

There is nothing worse the Lord endures at the hands of his people than when they think such hard thoughts of him. He knows full well what fruit this bitter root is likely to bear— what alienations of heart, what drawings back, what unbelief and turning away in our walk with him. How unwilling is a child to come into the presence of an angry father! Consider, then, this as of first importance: to receive from the Father as he holds out love to the soul. This gives him the honour he aims at and it is exceedingly acceptable to him. He often sets it out in an eminent manner that it may be so received. 'God shows his love for us' (Rom. 5:8). 'See what kind of love the Father has given to us' (1 John 3:1).

Where, then, does this folly of not trusting God's love come from? Men are afraid to have good thoughts of God. They think it a boldness to look on God as good, gracious, tender, kind, loving. I speak of saints. People judge him hard, austere, severe, almost implacable and fierce. They attribute to God the very worst affections of the very worst of men, and those most hated by God (Rom. 1:31; 2 Tim. 3:3). And think they are doing good when they think of God this way. Is not this deceit from Satan? Was it not his design from the beginning to inject into men's minds such thoughts of God?

Assure yourself, then, there is nothing more acceptable to the Father than for us to fill our hearts with thoughts of him as the eternal fountain of all that rich grace which flows out to sinners in the blood of Jesus.

2. We Delight in God When We Receive His Love by Faith

Receiving God's love by faith will be exceeding effective in making God dear to your soul, causing you to delight in him and make your home with him. Many saints have no greater burden in their lives than that their hearts do not come clearly, fully and constantly to delight and rejoice in God. As a result they are disinclined to walk closely with him. What is at the bottom of this malady? Is it not their lack of skill in, or neglect of, this duty, namely that of holding communion with the Father in love? The more we see of the love of God, the more we shall delight in him, and no more. Every other discovery of God, without this, will make the soul fly away from him. But if once the heart is taken up with the pre-eminence of the Father's love, it cannot choose but be overpowered, conquered and captivated by him. This alone will work upon us so that we make our home with him. If the love of a father will not make a child delight in him, what will?

Try this experiment, then: exercise your thoughts on this very thing: the eternal, free and fruitful love of the Father. And see if your hearts are not worked upon to delight in him. I boldly dare to say, believers will find it as thriving a course as ever they pitched on in their lives. Sit down a little at the fountain and you will quickly have a discovery more of the sweetness of the streams. You who have run from him will not be able, after a while, to keep at a distance for a moment.

Objection 1: But I Don't Know Whether God Loves Me

But some may say, 'Alas! How shall I have communion with the Father in love? I do not know at all whether he loves me or not so how shall I presume to cast myself upon his love? What if I am not accepted? Might I perish for my presumption rather than find sweetness in his bosom? God only seems to me to be a consuming fire and everlasting burnings so that I dread to look up unto him.'

Answer. You misunderstand what is involved in knowing the love of God. Though a sense of God's love might be carried on through spiritual experiences, yet it is received purely by believing. We know God loves us by believing in God's love as it is revealed. 'And we have known and believed the love that God has for us. God is love.' (1 John 4:16 NKJV) This is the assurance which, at the very entrance of walking with God, you may have of this love. He who is truth has said it. And whatever your heart says, or Satan says, unless you receive God's account, you make him a liar who has spoken it in his word (1 John 5:10).

Objection 2: But God Has No Reason to Love Me

Others may say: 'I can believe that God is love to others, for he has said he is love. But I see no grounds that persuade me that he will be loving to me. There is no cause, no reason in the world, why he should turn one thought of love or kindness towards me. And therefore I dare not cast myself upon his love, to hold communion with him.'

Answer. He has spoken it as particularly to you as to anyone in the world. And as for cause of love, he has as much cause to fix his love on you as on any of the children of men—that is, none at all without himself. So I shall make speedy work with this objection. No-one from the foundation of the world who believed such love in the Father and made returns of love to him again, was deceived. Neither shall anyone to the world's end ever be so deceived in so doing. You are, then, in this on a most sure foundation. If you believe and receive the Father as love, he will infallibly be so to you, though others may fall under his severity.

Objection 3: But My Heart Is Not Filled with Love for God

Some may say: 'I cannot find my heart responding to God's love. If I could I find my soul set on him, then I could believe his soul delighted in me.'

Answer. This is the most preposterous course that possibly your thoughts can pitch upon—a most ready way to rob God of his glory. 'This is love,' says the Holy Spirit, 'not that we have loved God but that he loved us' (1 John 4:10). Now, you would invert this order, and say, 'This is love, not that God loved me, but that I love him first.' This is to take the glory of God from him. Whereas he loves us without a cause that is in ourselves, and we have all cause in the world to love him, you would have the contrary. You assume there should be something in you for which God should love you —that is, your love to him. And you assume that you should love God before you know anything lovely in him—namely, whether he loves you or not. This course of action has been invented by the flesh. It will never bring glory to God, nor peace to your own soul. Lay down, then, your reasonings. Take up the love of the Father as a pure act of believing, and that will open your soul to the Lord in the communion of love.

Further Reading

John Owen's wordy prose and many digressions mean his books are not always easy going. But the Banner of Truth Trust has published a number of his works abridged and simplified by R. J. K. Law and Richard Rushing, and these are a delight to read.

- John Owen, *Communion with God* (Edinburgh: Banner of Truth, 2013).

- John Owen, *The Glory of Christ* (Edinburgh: Banner of Truth, 2009).

- John Owen, *The Holy Spirit* (Edinburgh: Banner of Truth, 2017).

- John Owen, *The Mortification of Sin* (Edinburgh: Banner of Truth, 2009).

- Sinclair B. Ferguson, *John Owen on the Christian Life* (Edinburgh: Banner of Truth, 1987).

- Matthew Barrett and Michael A. G. Haykin, *Owen on the Christian Life* (Wheaton, IL: Crossway, 2015).

8

RICHARD BAXTER
on Everyday Discipleship

RICHARD Baxter (1615–1691) was at his happiest telling people what to do. A natural leader, his was the voice that was heard in any gathering and he was the last to question his own contribution. He was a man who could irritate and even enrage others with direct (and sometimes tactless) speech. A nineteenth-century biographer noted sadly that, John Owen 'frequently made friends of enemies, while Baxter often made enemies of friends.'

Small wonder then, that when the ablest men of the church sat at Westminster to frame the essentials of the Reformed faith through the 1640s and early 1650s, Baxter was not invited. Still, Baxter took that disappointment in his stride and got on with what he did best, devoting himself to Christian ministry. His brilliant mind, apparently limitless energy, genius for organisation and deep desire for Christian unity, all left an indelible stamp upon the church of his time and the shape of future ministry. Go to Kidderminster in Worcestershire today, the focus of his pastoral ministry, and you can see a statue of Baxter. Baxter lived through the English Civil War, the rule of Cromwell's Parliament, the restoration of the monarchy and the outpouring of hostility against Puritan ministry, and survived it all. His *Autobiography* is a valuable historical source for this turbulent period and a window on Baxter's thought.

Called to Kidderminster in 1641, Baxter lamented its indifference to the Gospel, but persevered for almost twenty years with astonishing results. Armed with his Bible, prayer, an assistant at his side (whose needs Baxter largely met out of his own pocket), and a commanding and tenacious manner, Baxter saw a gospel revolution. Through preaching the ABC of the gospel week-by-week, unstinting house-to-house visiting and catechising, the town was steadily transformed. Many of Baxter's views on ministry are in his book *The Reformed Pastor*, a book which deserves to be read by every pastor.

Unlike many of his contemporaries, Baxter never had the privilege of a university education. But his self-directed course of studies and his natural intellectual brilliance meant he surpassed most of them in learning. Books (well over 150 of them), letters, sermons, tracts and treatises poured forth from his pen in such volume that scholars today have not fully caught up with his output.

Not all of Baxter's writings found him in orthodox company. Sometimes, and apparently out of zeal to build unity, he took wrong paths on theological issues. His views on the atonement and justification were well wide of the Reformed consensus of his day, and served to alienate Baxter from those with whom he might have worked more closely.

We are always on safe ground, though, when Baxter is our guide in pastoral matters. *The Saints' Everlasting Rest*, an extended meditation on heaven, was written when Baxter was still in his thirties. Its extreme length can make the book itself feel everlasting! But it is still read and appreciated today (usually in abridged versions).

Living in a large house next to the churchyard in Kidderminster were a wealthy widow and her teenage daughter, Margaret Charlton. Margaret was a proud, wealthy young woman with no gospel interest, until illness struck. Baxter committed himself to prayer and fasting that she might recover), and at some point after her recovery she came to a gospel faith. And then to everyone's astonishment, this single-minded and defiantly single minister fell in love with Margaret and they married in 1662. He was 47 and she was 26. Nineteen happy years of marriage followed until Margaret's death.[1]

What to Look Out For

Baxter published *The Christian Directory* in 1673—a giant of a book, running to 1,250,000 words. In the book he explores how the gospel is to be lived out in the heart, the home, the workplace, the church and the state. With no stone unturned, it set the benchmark for pastoral theology in its day, and remains both useful and readable in our times.

One of the key features of the Puritan vision was the application of the gospel to everyday life. Christian faith was not something to be confined to Sunday mornings or church gatherings. They expected the gospel to permeate their lives. In our extract Baxter leads us through twenty-four hours spent with God. What comes through is his desire to be practical and specific, while giving realistic and flexible counsel.

Baxter speaks of our 'calling'. This reflects the positive view that the Puritans had of our daily work as a vocation in which we are called to serve God. Baxter wrote in a pre-industrial era in which most work was carried out in the fields, houses or markets. So servants employed by wealthy householders are the nearest equivalent to believers today employed in offices and factories. Baxter has in his sights workers who share a faith together, but his words have much value for Christians seeking to be distinctive for Christ at work today.

Why turn to Baxter on the daily rhythms of work, rest and prayer, and workplace life? For all his skill in complex

[1] You can read Richard and Margaret Baxter's story in J. I. Packer, *A Grief Sanctified* (Wheaton, IL: Crossway, 1997).

theological arguments, Baxter excelled when speaking plain words to ordinary people. Let Baxter scrutinize *your* daily habits. What is he calling you to change? How is he drawing you to a closer walk with Christ?

❋

The Christian Directory

From Part 2, Chapter 17[2]

It helps to make a holy life more easy to us when we know the routines and method of our duties and everything falls into its proper place. It helps the farmer or tradesman to know the routines of his work, that he need not go out of it, except in extraordinary cases. Therefore I shall here give you some brief directions for the holy spending of every day.

Begin with Prayer

Proportion the time of your sleep aright, if it be in your power, so you do not waste your precious morning hours sluggishly in your bed. Let the time of your sleep be rationally fitted to your health and labour, and not sensually fitted to your slothful pleasure. About six hours is enough for healthy people and seven hours for the less healthy, and eight for the more weak and aged. The morning hours are the most precious of all the day for all our spiritual duties. Servants that are short of time must take time for prayer then if possible, lest they have none at all.

Let God have your first awaking thoughts. Lift up your hearts to him reverently and thankfully for the rest of the night past, and briefly cast yourselves upon him for the

---

[2] Richard Baxter, *A Christian Directory* (Grand Rapids: Soli Deo Gloria Publications, 2008), pp. 466-469.

following day. Get used to doing this so constantly that your consciences check you if, instead, common thoughts first intrude. And if you have a bed-fellow to speak to, let your first speech be agreeable to your thoughts. It will be a great help against the temptations that might otherwise surprise you and a help for a holy engagement of your hearts to God for all the day.

If more necessary duties do not call you away, let secret prayer by yourself alone or with your chamber-fellow (or both) go before the duties of the family and do not delay it. Let it be first before any other work of the day. Do not be formal and superstitious about your hours, as if God had absolutely tied you to such a time. Nor think it your duty to pray once in secret and once with your chamber-fellow and once with the family every morning when more necessary duties call you off. That hour is best for one which is worst for another. To most, private prayer works best as soon as they are up and clothed. But to others some other hour may be more free and fit. And those persons that have not more necessary duties may do well to pray at all the opportunities before mentioned.

Reading and reflection must be allowed their time also, and the labours of your callings must be attentively followed. Servants and poor people who are not at liberty or who have a need to provide for their families, may not lawfully take so much time for prayer as some others may. The aged and weak who cannot follow a calling may take longer time. And ministers that have many souls to look after and public work to do must take heed not to neglect any of this, so that they may be longer and more often in private prayer.

Always remember that when two duties are before you at the same time and one must be omitted, you must chose that which, all things considered, is the greater, so you must understand what makes a duty greater. Usually the greater duty is the one which tends to the greater good, yet sometimes the greater one is the one which cannot be done at another time. Praying in itself is better than ploughing or going to market or conversation, and yet these may be more important than prayer in their proper seasons, because prayer may be done at another time when these cannot.

Let family worship be performed constantly and seasonably twice a day at that hour which is most free from interruptions, not delaying it without just cause. But whenever it is performed, be sure it is reverently, seriously and spiritually done. Begin with a brief calling upon God's name and craving of his help and blessing through Christ. Then read some part of the Scripture in order, and either help the hearers to understand it and apply it or, if you are unable to do that, then read some profitable book to them for such ends. And sing a psalm (if there are enough to do it well), and earnestly pour out your souls in prayer. If unavoidable occasions will not give way to all this, do what you can, especially in prayer, and do the rest another time. But do not pretend something is a necessity that prevents you doing your duty when it is really unwillingness or negligence. Good times of family worship are a principal means of keeping up the power and cause of godliness in the world which decays when these grow dead and slight and formal.

Keep the End in View

Renew the intention of your actions and the remembrance of your ultimate end when you set yourselves to your day's work or set upon any notable business in the world. Let 'holiness to the Lord' be written upon your hearts in all that you do. Do no work which you cannot ascribe to God and truly say he set you about. Do nothing in the world for any other ultimate end than to please and glorify and enjoy him. And remember that, whatever you do, must be done as a means to these and as by one that is that way going on to heaven. All your labour must be like the labour of a traveller which is all for his journey's end. And all your respect or affection to any place or thing in your way must be in respect to your achieving your purpose, as a traveller loves a good way, a good horse, a good inn, a dry cloak, or good company. But nothing must be loved here as much as your end or home. Lift up your hearts to heaven and say, 'If this work and way did not tend directly or indirectly to it, then it is no work or way for me.' Whatever you do, do all to the glory of God (1 Cor. 10:31).

Hard at Work

Follow the labours of your calling carefully and diligently. From this will follow much profit.

1. You will show that you are not sluggish and a servant to your flesh as those that cannot deny its ease, and you will further the mortification of all fleshly lusts and desires which are fed by ease and idleness.

2. You will keep out idle thoughts from your mind which swarm in the minds of idle persons.

3. You will escape the loss of precious time which idle persons are daily guilty of.

4. You will be living obediently to God when the slothful are in a constant sin of omission.

5. You may have more time to spare for holy exercises if you follow your labour close when you are at it. Idle persons can have no time for prayer or reading because they lose it by loitering at their work, and leave their business uncompleted.

6. You may expect God's blessing for the provision for yourselves and your families, and to have something

to give to those in need when the slothful are in need themselves, and cast by their needs into an abundance of temptations and have nothing to do good with.

7. And it will also tend to the health of your bodies which will make them the fitter for the service of your souls, when slothfulness wastes time and health and estate and wit and grace and all.

Know Your Heart

Be thoroughly acquainted with your corruptions and temptations so you can watch against them all the day, especially the most dangerous sort of your corruptions and those temptations which your company or business will unavoidably lay before you. Be still watching and working against the great sins of unbelief, hypocrisy, selfishness, pride, sensuality or flesh-pleasing, and the inordinate love of earthly things. Take care, lest under pretence of diligence in your calling, you are drawn to earthly-mindedness and excessive cares, or to covetous designs for success in the world. If you are to trade or deal with others, take heed of selfishness, which desires to draw or save from others as much as you can for yourselves and your own advantage. Take heed of all that savours of injustice or uncharitableness in all your dealings with others.

- If you spend time with chatterers, guard against the temptation of idle talk. If you converse with angry persons, be fortified against their provocations.

- If you have conversations with lewd persons or such as are tempting those of the other sex, maintain that modesty and necessary distance and cleanness of speech which the laws of chastity require.

- If you have servants that are still faulty, take care, in

case their faults may make you faulty, and you may do something that is unseemly or unjust.

- If you are poor, watch out for the temptations of poverty, in case it brings upon you an evil far greater than itself.

- If you are rich, be most diligent in fortifying your hearts against those more dangerous temptations of riches which very few escape.

- If you have conversations with flatterers or those that much admire you, be fortified against swelling pride.

- If you have conversations with those that despise or injure you, be fortified against impatient, revengeful pride.

These works at first will be very difficult while sin is in any strength. But when you have got an habitual apprehension of the poisonous danger of every one of these sins and of the tendency of all temptations, your hearts will easily avoid them. You will avoid them without much tiring thoughtfulness and care, even as a man will pass by a house infected with the plague or go out of the way if he meet a cart or anything that would hurt him.

When you are alone in your labours, improve the time in practical, fruitful (not speculative and barren) meditations, especially in heart-work and heaven-work. Let your chief meditations be on the infinite goodness and perfections of God and the life of glory which in the love and praise of him you must live for ever. Let Christ and the mysteries of grace in man's redemption be the subject of your thoughts. If you are able to manage meditations methodically it will be best. But if you cannot do that without so much striving as will confound you and distract you and cast you into melancholy, it is better to let your meditations be in the form of shorter prayers. But let them usually be effective to do some good upon your hearts.

If you labour in company with others, be provided with skill, resolution and zeal to improve the time in profitable conversation and to avoid diversions.

Grow in Grace

Whatever you are doing, in company or alone, let the day be spent in the inward stimulation and exercise of the graces of the soul as well as in external bodily duties. And to that end, know that there is no external duty without internal grace to animate it, or else it is but an image or carcass and unacceptable to God. When you are praying and reading there are the graces of faith, repentance, etc., to be exercised there. When you are alone, meditation may help to actuate any grace as you find most needful. When are conferring with others you must exercise love to them, and love to that truth about which you confer, and other graces as the subject shall require. When you are provoked or under suffering, you have patience to exercise. But especially it must be your principal daily business by the exercise of faith to keep your hearts warm in the love of God and your dear Redeemer, and in the hopes and delightful thoughts of heaven.

There are various means of grace and they allow for deliberation and choice. For they are to be used but as means and not all at once. After deliberation and choice, you might sometimes use one and sometimes another for the same end. So all those graces which are but means must be used variously and with deliberation and choice. The love of God and of eternal life must be the constant tenor and constitution of the mind, as these are the ultimate graces which animate the exercise of every other intermediate grace. Never take up with bodily exercise alone, nor barren thoughts, unless your hearts are also employed in a course of duty and holy longing for God and love for him, or in the sincere internal part of the duty which you perform to men. Justice and love are graces which you must still exercise towards all that you have to deal with in the world. Love is called the fulfilling of the law (Rom. 13:10), because the love of God and man is the soul of every outward duty and a cause that will bring forth these as its effects.

Be aware of how you use your time, and every day be as careful not to waste your time as you not to waste your gold or silver. And if vain recreations, dressings, feastings, idle talk, unprofitable company or sleep be any of the temptations to rob you of any of your time, accordingly heighten your watchfulness and firm resolutions against them. Do not be more careful to escape thieves and robbers than to escape that person or action or course of life that would rob you of any of your time. And for the redeeming of time, especially see not only that you be never idle, but also that you be doing the greatest good that you can do and do not prefer a lesser good over a greater good.

Eating and Drinking

Eat and drink with temperance and thankfulness for health and not for unprofitable pleasure. For quantity, most carefully avoid excess, for many more exceed than take too little. Never please your appetite in meat or drink when it tends to the detriment of your health. 'It is not for kings to drink wine, or for rulers to take strong drink... Give strong drink to the one who is perishing, and wine to those in bitter distress' (Prov. 31:4-6). 'Woe to you O land when your king is a child and your princes eat in the morning. Blessed are you, O land, when your king is the son of nobles and your princes eat in due season for strength and not for drunkenness' (Eccles. 10:16-17). Poorer men must also take heed of intemperance and excess.

Let your diet incline rather to the coarser than the finer sort, and to the cheaper than the costly sort, and to sparing abstinence than to fulness. I would advise rich men especially to write in great letters on the walls of their dining rooms or parlours these two sentences: 'Behold, this was the guilt of your sister Sodom: she and her daughters had pride, excess of food, and prosperous ease, but did not aid the poor and needy' (Ezek. 16:49). 'There was a rich man who was clothed in purple and fine linen and who feasted sumptuously every day. … Child, remember that you in your lifetime received your good things' (Luke 16:19, 25). Paul wept when he mentioned them, whose end is destruction, whose god is their belly and whose glory is in their shame; who mind earthly things, being enemies to the cross (Phil. 3:18-19). O live not after the flesh, lest you die (Rom. 8:13; Gal. 6:8, 21, 23-24).

Stay Close to God and Man

If any temptation prevail against you and you fall into any sins besides common infirmities, presently lament it and confess not only to God but to men (when confession conduces more to good than harm), and rise by a true and thorough repentance immediately without delay. Spare not the flesh and daub not over the breach, and do not by excuses palliate the sore. Instead speedily rise to repentance, whatever it cost, for it will certainly cost you more to go on or to remain impenitent. And for your ordinary infirmities make not too light of them, but confess them and daily strive against them, and examine what strength you get against them, and do not aggravate them by impenitence and contempt.

Every day look to the special duties of your various relationships, whether you are husbands, wives, parents, children, masters, servants, pastors, people, magistrates, or subjects. Remember that every relationship has its special duty and its advantage for the doing of some good, and that God requires your faithfulness in these as well as in any other duty. Remember that in these a man's sincerity or hypocrisy is usually more tried than in any other parts of our lives.

Workplace Relationships

Love one another without pretence as yourselves. Avoid all arguing and falling out with one another, or anything that would weaken your love to one another, especially differences about your personal interests in point of profit, provision or reputation. Take heed of the spirit of envy which will make your hearts rise against those that are preferred before you, or that are used better than you. Remember the sin and misery of Cain, and take warning by him. Give place to others and in honour prefer others and seek not to be preferred before them (Rom. 12:10, 16). God delights to exalt the humble that abase themselves and to cast down those that exalt themselves. When the concerns of your earthly nature can make you hate or fall out with each other, what a fearful sign is it of an earthly mind (Rom. 8:6, 13).

Help one another with love and willingness in your labours. Do not bear grudges at one another, and say 'so-and-so does less than me'. Instead be as ready to help another as you would be helped yourselves. It is very amiable to see a family of such children and servants that all take one another's concerns as their own and are not selfish against each other. 'Behold, how good and pleasant it is when brothers dwell in unity' (Psa. 133:1).

Watch over one another for mutual preservation against the sin and temptations which you are most in danger of. Agree to tell each other of your faults, not proudly or passionately, but in love and resolve to take it thankfully from each other. If any one talks foolishly and idly or wantonly and immodestly, or tells a lie or take God's name in vain, or neglects their duty to God or man, or deals unfaithfully in their trust or labour, let the other seriously tell him of his sin and call him to repentance. And let not him that is guilty take it ill and angrily snap at the reproof, or justify or excuse the fault, but humbly thank him and promise amendment. Oh how happy might servants be if they would faithfully watch over one another.

Wholesome Talk

When you are together and your work will allow it, let your discourse be such as tends to edification and to the spiritual good of the speaker or the hearers. Some work there is that must be thought about and talked of while it is being done and will not allow you leisure to think or speak of other things till it is done. But very much of the work of most servants may be as well done, even though they think and speak together of heavenly things, besides all other times when their work is over. O take this time to be speaking of good to one another. It is likely that one of you has more knowledge than the rest. Let the rest be asking his counsel and instructions, and let him bend himself to do them good. Or if you are equal in knowledge, you can stir up the grace that is in you if you have any or stir up your desire for grace if you have none.

Waste not your precious time in vanity. Do not multiply the sin of idle words. Oh what a load lies on many a soul that does not feel the guilt of these two sins, loss of time and idle words. To be guilty of the same sins over and over every day and make a constant practice of them, and this against your own knowledge and conscience, is a more grievous case than many think. If you would live together as the heirs of heaven and provoke one another to the love of God and holy duty and delightfully talk of the word of God and the life to come, what blessings might you be to one another. Your service and labour would be a sanctified and comfortable life to you all.

'Let no corrupting talk come out of your mouths, but only such as is good for building up, as fits the occasion, that it may give grace to those who hear. And do not grieve the Holy Spirit of God' (Eph. 4:29-30). 'But sexual immorality and all impurity or covetousness must not even be named among you, as is proper among saints. Let there be no filthiness nor foolish talk nor crude joking, which are out of place, but instead let there be thanksgiving' (Eph. 5:3-4).

Patiently bear with the failings of one another towards yourselves, and hide those faults the opening up of which would do no good but stir up strife. But do not conceal those faults which will be cherished by concealment or whose concealment tends to the wrong of your master or any other. For it is in your power to forgive a fault against yourselves, but not against God or another. And to know when you should reveal it and when not you must wisely foreknow, ask yourself which way is likely to do more good or harm. So if you are in doubt, open it first to some secret friend who is wise to advise you whether it should be further opened or not.

If weakness or sickness or want afflict a brother or sister or fellow servant be kind and helpful to them, according to your power. Love not in word only but in deed and truth (1 John 3:18; James 2).

Let your speech be seasonable when wisdom tells you it is likely to do more harm than good. There is a season for the prudent to be silent and refrain even from good talk (Amos 5:17; Psa. 39:1-2). 'Cast not pearls before swine and give not holy things to dogs that you know will turn again and rend you' (cf. Matt. 7:6). Indeed, among good people themselves there is a time to speak and a time to be silent (Eccles. 3:7). There may possibly be such excess as tends to the tiring of the hearers, and more may be crammed in than they can digest and surfeiting may make them loathe it afterwards. You must give no more than they can bear, and also the matters of your business and callings must be talked of in their time and place.

Let all your speech of holy things be with the greatest seriousness and reverence that you are able. Let the words be never so good that levity and rudeness may make them to be profane. God and holy things should not be talked of in a common manner, but the gravity of your speech should tell the hearers that you take them not for small or common matters. If servants and others that live near together would converse and speak as the very words of God how holy and heavenly and happy would such families or societies be!

Finish the Day Well

In the evening return to the worshipping of God in the family and in secret as was directed for the morning. And do all with seriousness as in the sight of God and in the sense of your necessities. Make it your delight to receive instructions from the Holy Scripture and praise God and call upon his name through Christ.

If you have any extraordinary obstacles one day to hinder you in your duty to God and man, make it up by diligence the next. And if you have any extraordinary helps make use of them and let them not overcome you. If it is a day for a special sermon, or there is a funeral sermon, or you have opportunity to speak with men of extraordinary worth, or if it is a day of humiliation or thanksgiving, it may be that you could gather a double measure of strength by such extraordinary helps.

Before you go to sleep it is ordinarily a safe and needful course to take a review of the actions and mercies of the past day. In this way, you may be specially thankful for all special mercies and humbled for sins. You may renew your repentance and resolutions for obedience. You may examine yourselves to see whether your souls are growing better or worse, and whether sin goes down and grace increases, and whether you are any better prepared for sufferings and death. But do not waste too much time in the ordinary accounts of your life, like those who neglect their duty while they are examining how they perform duty and perplexing themselves with the deep consideration of their ordinary weaknesses. But by a general yet sincere repentance bewail your unavoidable daily failings and have recourse to Christ for a daily pardon and renewed grace. In the case of extraordinary sins or mercies be sure to be extraordinarily humbled or thankful.

Some think it best to keep a daily catalogue or diary of their sins and mercies. If you do so, do not be too particular in the enumeration of those that are the matter of every day's return. For it will become a temptation to waste your time and neglect greater duty. It may make you grow customary and unaware of such sins and mercies when they come to be recited over and over from day to day. But let the common mercies be more generally recorded and the common sins generally confessed, yet neither of them therefore slighted. Let the extraordinary mercies and greater sins have a more particular observation. Yet remember that sins and mercies which it is not fit that others be acquainted with are more safely committed to memory than to writing, and a well-humbled and a thankful heart should not easily let the memory of them slip.

When you compose yourselves to sleep, again commit yourselves to God through Christ and crave his protection. Close up the day with some holy exercise of faith and love. And if you are persons that must lie awake in the night, let your meditations be holy and exercised upon that subject that is most profitable to your souls. But I cannot give this as an ordinary direction because the body must have sleep or else it will be unfit for labour. And all thoughts of holy things must be serious and all serious thoughts will hinder sleep. Those that wake in the night do so unwillingly, and would not put themselves out of hopes of sleep, which such serious meditations would do. Nor can I advise you ordinarily to rise in the night to prayer as some papists have vowed to do. For this is but to serve God with irrational and hurtful ceremony. It is a wonder how far such men will go in ceremony that will not be drawn to a life of love and spiritual worship. If men did not irrationally place the service of God in praying this hour rather than another, they might see how improvidently and sinfully they lose their time in twice dressing and undressing and in the intervals of their sleep, when they might spare all that time by sitting the longer or rising the earlier for the same employment. Besides, what tendency it hath to the destruction of health by cold and interruption of necessary rest when God approves not of the disabling of the body or destroying our health or shortening life no more than of murder or cruelty to others. Instead God, only calls us to deny our unnecessary sensual delights and use the body so as it may be most serviceable to the soul and him.

I have briefly laid together these directions for the right spending of every day that those that need them and cannot remember the larger more particular directions may at least get these few engraven on their minds and make them the daily practice of their lives. If you will sincerely do this then you cannot conceive how conducive it will be to the holiness, fruitfulness, and quietness of your lives, and to your peaceful and comfortable death.

Further Reading

- Richard Baxter, *The Reformed Pastor* (Edinburgh: Banner of Truth, 2012).

- Richard Baxter, *Anger Management*, an extract from *A Christian Directory*, adapted by Richard Rushing (Edinburgh: Banner of Truth, 2008).

- Richard Baxter, *A Christian Directory* (Grand Rapids: Soli Deo Gloria Publications, 2008).

- Richard Baxter, *The Saints' Everlasting Rest* (Vancouver: Regent College Publishing, 2004).

- Richard Baxter, *The Pastor's Pastor: Autobiography* (Fearn, Ross-shire: Christian Focus, 2001).

- J. I. Packer, *A Grief Sanctified* (Wheaton, IL: Crossway, 1997).

9

JOHN BUNYAN
on Faith

'FOR two centuries *Pilgrim's Progress* was the best-read book, after the Bible, in all Christendom, but sadly it is not so today.' So says J. I. Packer. 'The time is ripe,' he continues, 'for us to dust off *Pilgrim's Progress* and start reading it again. Certainly, it would be great gain for modern Christians if Bunyan's masterpiece came back into its own in our day.'[1]

The Pilgrim's Progress was written by John Bunyan (1628-1688). Bunyan was born into a poor family in Elstow, near Bedford, and fought for the Parliamentary Army in the English Civil War. After the war he returned to Elstow and took up his father's trade as a tinker, a mender of pots and pans. Bunyan was a Baptist and was imprisoned for extended periods for his preaching.

King Charles II once asked John Owen why he went to hear the preaching of an uneducated tinker. Owen had been a chaplain to Oliver Cromwell, Vice-chancellor of Oxford University and remains one of England's greatest theologians. Yet Owen replied, 'May it please your Majesty, could I possess

---

[1] J. I. Packer, 'Pilgrim's Progress *The Devoted Life: An Invitation to the Puritan Classics*, ed. Kapic and Gleason (Downer's Grove, IL: InterVarsity Press, 2004), p. 198.

the tinker's ability for preaching, I would willingly relinquish all my learning.'[2]

Pilgrim's Progress is an allegorical narrative that uses the conceit of a dream to present the story of conversion and discipleship. The lead character is called 'Christian'. Christian has found a book (the Law), and having read it he is now in spiritual anguish because he carries a terrible burden (his sin). The book says his home town, the City of Destruction, will be destroyed, but that there is another city, the Celestial City, and Christian longs to get there, despite opposition and ridicule from friends and family. He doesn't know the way, however, until he meets a man named Evangelist, who sets him off on the right course.

Christian is later joined by Hopeful. At one point the two pilgrims take shelter in the grounds of Doubting Castle where they awake to the threats of the castle's owner, the Giant Despair. Christian and Hopeful only escape when they remember they possess the key of Promise which unlocks any door in Despair's castle.

Things to Look Out For

The Puritans believed that coming to Christ in faith was normally preceded by a period of conviction of sin. We need a God-given awareness of our plight before we look for a solution. Bunyan's story of Christian forms a kind of case study of this process. The key thing when people are feeling the weight of their sin is that they seek the solution in the right place. So Bunyan powerfully expresses the dangers of numbing our sense of need with the false solutions offered by formal religion or moral self-improvement. Only coming to the cross of Christ genuinely sets us free.

Bunyan also shows how faith is not just the act by which we first become Christians. What keeps us on track as we head towards our final goal is faith in the promises of God.

[2] Andrew Thomson, *John Owen, Prince of Puritans* (Fearn, Ross-shire: Christian Focus, 1996), p. 54.

The language of pilgrimage and journey remain common today. 'We are all on a journey', we are often told. Or we are encouraged to embrace 'fellow travellers', even if we are at different places on our journey. When people use the language of journey in this way (sometimes even co-opting Bunyan to their cause), they do so to stress the provisionality of destination and thereby justify deviating from biblical orthodoxy. But the pilgrim of *Pilgrim's Progress* knew where he was going. His goal was never in doubt. He is heading to the Celestial City. And the only way to get there was through confidence in the word and reliance of Christ. Indeed the narrow gate of *Pilgrim's Progress* is precisely an image of the exclusive claims of Christ.

✻

Pilgrim's Progress [3]

Christian Leaves the City of Destruction

As I walked through the wilderness of this world, I found a certain place where was a den, and laid down in that place to sleep. And as I slept, I dreamed a dream. I dreamed, and behold, I saw a man clothed with rags, standing in a certain place, with his face from his own house, a book in his hand, and a great burden upon his back. I looked and saw him open the book and read therein. And as he read, he wept and trembled. And not being able to contain himself any longer, he broke out with a lamentable cry, saying, 'What shall I do?'

In this plight, therefore, he went home, and restrained himself as long as he could, so that his wife and children should not perceive his distress. But he could not be silent long, because his trouble increased. So at length he spoke

---

[3] John Bunyan, *The Pilgrim's Progress* (Edinburgh: Banner of Truth, 1977), pp. 1-4, 11-20, 35-36, 129-135.

of what was on his mind to his wife and children. Thus he began to talk to them: 'O, my dear wife,' said he, 'and you the children of my heart, I, your dear friend, am in myself undone by reason of a burden that lies heavy upon me. Moreover, I am certainly informed that this our city will be burnt with fire from heaven. In this fearful overthrow, both myself, with you my wife and you my sweet babes, shall miserably come to ruin, except (in a way I see not) some escape can be found whereby we may be delivered.'

At this his relations were sore amazed. It was not that they believed that what he had said to them was true, but because they thought that some frenzied distemper had got into his head. Therefore, as it was drawing towards night, and hoping that sleep might settle his brains, with all haste they put him to bed. But the night was as troublesome to him as the day. Therefore, instead of sleeping, he spent it in sighs and tears.

So, when the morning was come, they asked how he was. He told them, 'Worse and worse.' He also started talking to them again. But they began to be hardened. They also thought to drive away his distemper by harsh and surly treatment. Sometimes they would deride him, sometimes they would chide him, and sometimes they would quite neglect him. Therefore he began to retire to his room to pray for them and for comfort for his own misery. He would also walk on his own in the fields, sometimes reading, and sometimes praying. Thus for some days he spent his time.

Now I saw, upon a time, when he was walking in the fields, that he was (as was his habit) reading in his book, and greatly distressed in his mind. And as he read, he burst out, as he had done before, crying, 'What shall I do to be saved?' I saw also that he looked this way and that way as if he would run. Yet he stood still because (as I perceived) he could not tell which way to go.

I looked then and saw a man named *Evangelist* coming to him, and he asked, 'Why do you cry?' He answered, 'Sir, I perceive by the book in my hand that I am condemned to die and after that to come to judgment. And I find that I am not willing to do the first, nor able to do the second.'

Then said *Evangelist*, 'Why not willing to die, since this life is accompanied by so many evils?' The man answered, 'Because I fear that this burden that is upon my back will sink me lower than the grave, and I shall fall into the pit of fire. And Sir, if I be not fit to go to prison, I am not fit to go to judgment, and from there to execution. Thinking about these things makes me cry.'

Then said *Evangelist*, 'If this be your condition, why do you stand still?' He answered, 'Because I know not where to go.' Then *Evangelist* gave him a parchment roll and there was written within, 'Fly from the wrath to come.'

The man therefore read it and looking upon *Evangelist* very carefully said, 'Where must I fly?' Then said *Evangelist* (pointing with his finger over a very wide field), 'Do you see yonder wicket-gate?' The man said, 'No.' Then said the other, 'Do you see yonder shining light?' He said, 'I think I do.' Then said *Evangelist*, 'Keep that light in your eye, and go up directly there, so shall you see the gate. At the gate, when you knock, you will be told what you should do.'

So I saw in my dream that the man began to run. Now he had not run far from his own door when his wife and children, perceiving it, began to cry after him to return. But the man put his fingers in his ears, and ran on crying, 'Life! Life! Eternal life!' He looked not behind him, but fled towards the middle of the plain ...

Worldly Wiseman Persuades Christians to Head for the House of Mr Legality

Mr Worldly Wiseman said to *Christian:* How now, good fellow, where are you going in this burdened manner?

Christian: A burdened manner indeed as ever I think poor creature had! And as for your question, Where are you going? I tell you, sir, I am going to yonder wicket-gate before me. For there, as I am informed, I shall be shown a way to be rid of my heavy burden.

Mr Worldly Wiseman: Have you a wife and children?

Christian: Yes; but I am so laden with this burden that I cannot take that pleasure in them as formerly I do. So I think I am as if I had none.

Mr Worldly Wiseman: Will you listen to me, if I give you counsel?

Christian: If it be good, I will, for I stand in need of good counsel.

Mr Worldly Wiseman: I would advise you, then, that with all speed you rid yourself of your burden. For you will never be settled in your mind till then. Nor can you enjoy the benefits of the blessings which God has bestowed upon you till then.

Christian: That is what I seek, even to be rid of this heavy burden. But I cannot get it off myself, nor is there any man in our country that can take it off my shoulders. Therefore I am going this way, as I told you, that I may be rid of my burden.

Mr Worldly Wiseman: Who told you to go this way to be rid of your burden?

Christian: A man that appeared to me to be a very great and honourable person. His name, as I remember, is Evangelist.

Mr Worldly Wiseman: I curse him for his counsel! There is not a more dangerous and troublesome way in the world than that into which he has directed you. And that is what you shall find if you are ruled by his counsel. You have met with problems already, as I perceive, for I see the dirt of the Slough of Despond is upon you. But that slough is just the beginning of the sorrows that accompany those that go on in that way. Hear me. I am older than you. You are likely to meet in the way which you're going with wearisomeness, painfulness, hunger, perils, nakedness, sword, lions, dragons, darkness, and, in a word, death, and what not. These things are certainly true having been confirmed by many testimonies. And should a man so carelessly cast away himself by giving heed to a stranger?

Christian: Why, sir, this burden on my back is more terrible to me than are all these things which you have mentioned. Indeed, I care not what I meet with in the way, if I can also meet with deliverance from my burden.

Mr Worldly Wiseman: How did you come by thy burden at first?

Christian: By reading this book in my hand.

Mr Worldly Wiseman: I thought so. What has happened to you has happened to other weak men, who, meddling with things too high for them, suddenly fall into your distractions. These distractions not only unman men, as your distractions I perceive have done to you, but they drive them towards desperate ventures to obtain they know not what.

Christian: I know what I would obtain: it is ease from my heavy burden.

Mr Worldly Wiseman: But why will you seek for ease this way, seeing so many dangers attend it? Especially since (had you but patience to hear me) I could direct you to the obtaining of what you desire without the dangers that you will run into in this way. For the remedy is at hand. Besides, I will add that, instead of those dangers, you shall meet with much safety, friendship and content.

Christian: Sir, I pray open this secret to me.

Mr Worldly Wiseman: Why, in yonder village (the village is named Morality) there dwells a gentleman whose name is *Legality,* a very judicious man, and a man of a very good name. He has the skill to help men get rid of such burdens as yours from their shoulders. Indeed, to my knowledge, he has done a great deal of good this way. And besides, he has the skill to cure those that are somewhat crazed in their wits with their burdens. To him, as I said, you may go and be helped presently. His house is not quite a mile from this place. And if he should not be at home himself, he has a handsome young son whose name is *Civility,* that can do it as well as the old gentleman himself. There, I say, you may be eased of your burden. And if you are not minded to go back to your former home (as indeed I would not wish you) you may send for your wife and children so they can come to this village. For there are houses now standing empty, one of which you may have at a reasonable rate. Provision there is also cheap and good. That which will make your life more happy is in credit and good fashion. And to be sure you shall live there alongside honest neighbours.

Now *Christian* was undecided. But eventually he concluded, If what this gentleman has said is true, then my wisest course is to take his advice. And with that he thus spoke again.

Christian: Sir, which is my way to this honest man's house?

Mr Worldly Wiseman: Do you see yonder high hill?

Christian: Yes, very well.

Mr Worldly Wiseman: By that hill you must go, and the first house you come to is his.

So *Christian* turned off his way to go to Mr *Legality*'s house for help. But, behold, when he got close to the hill, it seemed so high. And the side of the hill that was next the path loomed over it so that *Christian* was afraid to venture further in case the hill should fall on his head. So there he stood still, not knowing what to do. His burden now seemed heavier to him than while he was on his way. There came also flashes of fire out of the hill that made *Christian* afraid that he should be burnt. Here therefore he sweated and quaked for fear. And now he began to be sorry that he had taken Mr *Worldly Wiseman*'s counsel.

And with that he saw *Evangelist* coming to meet him, at the sight of whom he began to blush for shame. So *Evangelist* drew nearer and nearer. Coming up to *Christian*, *Evangelist* looked upon him with a severe and dreadful countenance …

Then said *Evangelist* … 'Now the just shall live by faith; but if any man draw back, my soul shall have no pleasure in him.' He also thus applied these words: You are the man that is running into this misery. You have begun to reject the counsel of the Most High, and to draw back your foot from the way of peace, even at the risk of your damnation.

Then *Christian* fell down at his feet as dead, crying, 'Woe is me, for I am undone!' At the sight of this *Evangelist* caught him by the right hand, saying, 'All manner of sin and blasphemies shall be forgiven unto men.' 'Do not be faithless, but believing.' Then *Christian* revived a little again, and stood up trembling, as at first, before *Evangelist*.

Then *Evangelist* proceeded, saying, Give more earnest heed to the things that I shall tell you. I will now show you who it was that deluded you and who it was also to whom he sent you. The man that met you is one *Worldly Wiseman*, and rightly is he so called. Partly this is because he savours only the doctrine of this world (therefore he always goes to the town of *Morality* to church). And partly this is because he loves that doctrine best, for it saves him best from the cross. And partly it is because he is of this carnal temper which means he seeks to pervert my ways, though they are right. Now there are three things in this man's counsel that you must utterly abhor. First, his turning you away from the way. Second, his labouring to render the cross odious to you. And third, his setting your feet in that way that leads to the administration of death …

He to whom you were sent for ease, the one named *Legality,* is the son of the bond-woman who is now in bondage with her children. She represents, in mysterious way, this Mount Sinai which you feared would fall on your head. Now if she with her children are in bondage, how can you expect to be made free by them? This *Legality,* therefore, is not able to set you free from your burden. No man ever got rid of his burden by Legality. No, nor ever is likely to be. You cannot be justified by the works of the law; for by the deeds of the law no man living can be rid of his burden. Therefore Mr *Worldly Wiseman* is an alien, Mr *Legality* is a cheat, and his son *Civility,* notwithstanding his simpering looks, is but a hypocrite. They cannot help you. Believe me, there is nothing in all this noise that you have heard from these drunkards, but a design to cheat you of your salvation, by turning you from the way in which I had set you.

After this, *Evangelist* called aloud to the heavens for confirmation of what he had said. And with that there came words and fire out of the mountain under which poor *Christian* stood, which made the hair of his flesh stand up. The words were pronounced: 'As many as are of the works of the law are under the curse. For it is written, Cursed is every one that does not continue in all things which are written in the book of the law to do them.'

Now *Christian* looked for nothing but death, and began to cry out lamentably. He cursed the time in which he met with Mr *Worldly Wiseman* and called himself a thousand fools for hearkening to his counsel. He also was greatly ashamed to think that this gentleman's arguments, flowing only from the flesh, should have prevailed with him so far as to cause him to forsake the right way. This done, he applied himself again to *Evangelist* in words and sense as follows.

Christian: Sir, what think you? Is there any hope? May I now go back, and go up to the wicket-gate? Shall I not be abandoned for this, and sent back from here ashamed? I am sorry I hearkened to this man's counsel. But may my sin be forgiven?

Then said *Evangelist* to him: Your sin is very great, for by it you have committed two evils: you have forsaken the way that is good and you have walked along forbidden paths. Yet the man at the gate will receive you, for he has good-will for men. Only, said *Evangelist,* take heed that you turn not aside again, or else you will 'perish from the way, when his wrath is kindled but a little' …

Christian Loses His Burden at the Hill with a Cross

Now I saw in my dream that the highway up which *Christian* was to go was fenced on either side with a wall and that wall was called *Salvation*. Up this way, therefore, did burdened *Christian* run, but not without great difficulty because of the load on his back.

He ran thus till he came at a place somewhat ascending. And on that place stood a cross and a little below, at the bottom, a sepulchre. So I saw in my dream that, just as Christian came up with the cross, his burden loosed from off his shoulders and fell from off his back. It began to tumble, and continued to do so until it came to the mouth of the sepul-chre, where it fell in, and I saw it no more.

Then was *Christian* glad and light-hearted, and said with a merry heart, 'He has given me rest by his sorrow and life by his death.' Then he stood still a while to look and wonder. For it was very surprising to him that the sight of the cross should thus ease him of his burden. He looked, therefore, and looked again, until the springs that were in his head sent the waters down his cheeks.

Now, as he stood looking and weeping, behold, three Shin-ing Ones came to him, and saluted him with, 'Peace be to you.' The first said to him, 'Your sins are forgiven you.' The second stripped him of his rags and clothed him with change of raiment. The third also set a mark on his forehead, and gave him a roll with a seal upon it. He bid *Christian* look on the roll as he ran and told him to give it in at the celestial gate. So they went their way. Then *Christian* gave three leaps for joy, and went on singing,

> Thus far did I come laden with my sin,
> and nothing eased the grief that I was in,
> till I came hither. What a place is this!
> Must here be the beginning of my bliss?
> Must here the burden fall from off my back?
> Must here the strings that bound it to me crack?
> Blest cross! Blest sepulchre! Blest rather be
> the Man that there was put to shame for me!

Christian and Hopeful are Imprisoned by Giant Despair in Doubting Castle

Now Giant *Despair* had a wife, and her name was *Diffidence*. When Giant *Despair* went to bed he told his wife what he had done: how he had taken a couple of prisoners and cast them into his dungeon for trespassing on his grounds. Then he asked her what should be done to them. So she asked him who they were, where they came from and where they were bound. Then she counselled him that when he arose in the morning he should beat them without mercy. So when he arose, he got himself a grievous crab-tree cudgel, and went down into the dungeon to them. There he first berated them as if they were dogs, although they gave him never a word of distaste. Then he fell upon them, beating them fearfully, in such as way that they were not able to help themselves or to turn away on the floor. This done, he withdrew and left them there to console their misery and to mourn under their distress. So all that day they spent the time in nothing but sighs and bitter lamentations.

The next night, she, talking with her husband further about them, and understanding that they were still alive, advised him to counsel them to do away with themselves. So when morning was come, he went to them in a surly manner, as before, and found them to be very sore with the stripes that he had given them the day before. He told them that, since they were never likely to come out of that place, their only way forward would be to make an end of themselves, either with knife, noose or poison. 'For why', he said, 'should you choose to live, seeing that life is accompanied by so much bitterness?' But they asked him to let them go. With that he gave them an ugly look and rushed towards. He would had doubtless made an end of them himself, but he fell into one of his fits (for sometimes in sunny weather he fell into fits) and lost the use of his hands for a time. So he withdrew and left them as before to consider what to do. Then the prisoners consulted between themselves whether it was best to take his counsel or not ... Now *Christian* seemed for doing it, but *Hopeful* made his reply as follows:

Hopeful: 'My brother,' said he, 'do you remember not how

valiant you have been so far? Apollyon could not crush you, nor could all that you heard or saw or felt in the Valley of the Shadow of Death. What hardship, terror and amazement you have already gone through. And are you now nothing but fears! You see that I am in the dungeon with you, a far weaker man by nature than you are. This giant has wounded me as well as you, and has also cut off the bread and water from my mouth, and with you I mourn without the light. But let us exercise a little more patience. Remember how you played the man at Vanity Fair, and were neither afraid of the chain nor cage, nor even of bloody death. Therefore let us (at least to avoid the shame that it becomes not a Christian to be found in) bear up with patience as well as we can.'

Now, night being come again and the giant and his wife being in bed, she asked him about the prisoners and if they had taken his counsel. To this he replied, 'They are sturdy rogues; they choose rather to bear all hardships than to make away with themselves.' Then she said, 'Take them into the castle-yard tomorrow and show them the bones and skulls of those that you have already dispatched. Make them believe, before a week comes to an end, you will tear them in pieces, as you have done their fellows before them.'

So when the morning was come, the giant went to them again, and took them into the castle-yard and showed them as his wife had suggested. 'These', said he, 'were once pilgrims, as you are, and they trespassed on my grounds, as you have done. And when I thought fit I tore them in pieces. And so within ten days I will do you. Get down to your den again.' And with that he beat them all the way there. They lay, therefore, all day on Saturday in a lamentable case as before.

Now, when night was come, and when Mrs *Diffidence* and her husband the giant had gone to bed, they began to renew their discussion of their prisoners. And the old giant wondered how it was that he could neither by his blows nor counsel bring them to an end. And with that his wife replied, 'I fear that they live in hopes that someone will come to relieve them; or that they have pick-locks about them by the means of which they hope to escape.' 'Do you think so?' said the giant. 'I will therefore search them in the morning.'

Well, on Saturday about midnight they began to pray and continued in prayer till almost break of day.

Now a little before it was day, good *Christian,* as one half amazed, broke into this passionate speech: 'What a fool I am,' he said, 'to lie in a stinking dungeon like this, when I can walk at liberty! I have a key in my bosom called *Promise* that will, I am persuaded, open any lock in *Doubting Castle.*' Then said *Hopeful,* 'That is good news. Good brother, pluck it out of your bosom, and try.'

Then *Christian* pulled it out of his bosom and began to try at the dungeon-door. As he turned the key, the bolt drew back and the door flew open with ease. And *Christian* and *Hopeful* both came out. Then he went to the outer door that leads into the castle-yard and with his key opened that door also. After he went to the iron gate, for that must be opened too. That lock was desperately hard, yet the key opened it. They then thrust open the gate to make their escape with speed. But that gate, as it opened, made such a creaking, that it wakened *Giant Despair.* Hastily rising to pursue his prisoners, the giant felt his limbs fail for his fits took him again. So there was no way he could go after them. Then they went on and came to the King's highway and so were safe, because they were out of his jurisdiction.

Now, when they were gone over the stile, they began to plan together what they should do at that stile to prevent those that came after them from falling into the hands of *Giant Despair.* So they agreed to erect there a pillar and to engrave upon the side of it this sentence: 'Over this stile is the way to *Doubting Castle* which is kept by *Giant Despair,* who despises the King of the Celestial country and who seeks to destroy his holy pilgrims.' Many, therefore, that followed after them read what was written and escaped the danger. This done, they sang as follows:

> Out of the way we went, and then we found
> what 'twas to tread upon forbidden ground.
> And let them that come after have a care,
> lest heedlessness makes them as we to fare;
> lest they, for trespassing, his prisoners are,
> whose castle's Doubting and whose name's Despair.

Further Reading

- John Bunyan, *Pilgrim's Progress* (Edinburgh: Banner of Truth, 2017).

- John Bunyan, *Prayer* (Edinburgh: Banner of Truth, 2012).

- John Bunyan, *All Loves Excelling* (Edinburgh: Banner of Truth, 1998).

- *The Works of John Bunyan,* 3 vols. (Edinburgh: Banner of Truth, 2009).

- Faith Cook, *Fearless Pilgrim: The Life and Times of John Bunyan* (Darlington: Evangelical Press, 2008).

10

JOHN FLAVEL
on Providence

I N 1656, John Flavel went as a minister to Dartmouth in Devon. It was a town made wealthy by fishing and strategically important to the English fleet due to its deep-water harbour. Flavel fell in love with the place and its people. For thirty-five years he resisted calls to pastor elsewhere as well as the opposition of the authorities in order to serve God in the area.

John Flavel (1627-1691) was the son of a gospel minister who came to faith when he was studying at University College, Oxford, most likely in 1648. From Oxford he went in 1650 to Diptford in Devon as an assistant pastor. It was six fruitful years later, and after losing his first wife and remarrying, that Flavel was called to Dartmouth. He got to work preaching, visiting the sick, studying, and writing. Among his first works were sermons devoted to the needs of the local seafarers (*Navigation Spiritualized: A New Compass for Seamen* and *A Faithful Narrative of Some Late and Wonderful Sea Deliverances*—both highly readable).

In 1662 King Charles II introduced the Act of Uniformity, designed to expel evangelical ministers from the Church of England. Flavel was one of more than two thousand who refused to comply with these measures. For most of the next ten years he was effectively banned from Dartmouth, but exercised a courageous (and often clandestine) ministry in the area, sometimes slipping into the town in disguise in order to preach and to encourage believers.

Even when Flavel was allowed back into the town in 1672, he faced harassment and opposition. As public ministry was increasingly difficult, Flavel spent his time writing, and thereby left a legacy to future believers. Three of Flavel's most important works were written during this time. *The Fountain of Life* (1673) is a series of sermons on the Person and Work of Christ. This was followed by a sequel, *The Method of Grace* (1681), a sermon series exploring how God redeems sinners through Christ and then sanctifies them by his Spirit.

Flavel decided that a period in London might give him more freedom for preaching, and for two years he lived and worked there. He lost his second wife, and married again for the last time. Yet eventually, although offered a pastorate in the capital, Flavel declined and returned to his beloved Dartmouth.

There was no let-up in the trials Flavel was to face there. House arrest and three years of severe restrictions followed. But then in 1689, non-conformists were given more freedoms. For the last four years of Flavel's life he was able to work freely, and devoted himself to his greatest concerns, the building up of believers and developing unity between churches.

Flavel was dearly loved in his day and his writings have continued to have an impact after his death (in particular, on the American preacher and theologian Jonathan Edwards). Flavel writes with a pastor's heart, giving practical advice with love and respect.

Things to Look Out For

The times Flavel lived in appear to be so different from ours, with a slow-paced pre-industrial life, and a shared Christian outlook. Look beneath the surface, though, and our age and

Flavel's have many points of overlap. Now, just as then, true Christianity is increasingly despised, with evangelicals on the receiving end of hostility and suspicion. Society around us is changing rapidly. Nothing looks certain, and we may even wonder if the gospel really is God's life-transforming message for the world.

In this climate believers are tempted to do two things: we can indulge in nostalgia, longing for the 'good old days' when the church was stronger; or we can be consumed with fear and discouragement, doubting that God is with us at all. Each is a dangerous path, and if we indulge those desires, we'll lose our edge, and maybe, our faith.

Flavel brings us the remedy. The hardest season of Flavel's life produced his best-known work, *Divine Conduct,* or *The Mystery of Providence* (1678), a series of sermons on Psalm 57:2. The word 'providence' describes God's involvement in the world and our lives for his glory and for our good. Flavel says 'there are two ways whereby the blessed God condescends to manifest Himself to men: His word and his works.' It is through the works of providence, in other words, that we see God in his world. The key doctrine of the text is that it is our duty to trace God's providence in his dealings with us. In such times we need to strengthen our faith with both the word of God and the work of God in our lives. That means, fighting busyness and distraction, we must learn to reflect on our lives and look for signs of God's grace.

❋

The Mystery of Providence

From Chapter 9—How to Meditate on the Providence of God[1]

> I cry out to God Most High, to God,
> who fulfils his purpose for me.
>
> *Psalm 57:2*

Look for Signs of God's Providence

Labour to get as full and thorough recognition of the providences of God about you as you are able. Fill your hearts with the thoughts of him and his ways. If a single act of providence is so wonderful, what would many such be, if they were presented together to the view of the soul? If one star is so beautiful to behold, what is a constellation! Let your reflections, therefore, upon the acts and workings of providence for you, be full.

Let them be as extensively full, as may be. Search back into all the workings of providence throughout your lives. This is what Asaph did in Psalm 77:11-12: 'I will remember the deeds of the LORD; yes, I will remember your wonders of old. I will ponder all your work, and meditate on your mighty deeds.' He laboured to bring to mind all the ancient providences of God's mercies over many years past, and taste a fresh sweetness in them by new reflections on them. Let me tell you, there is not such a pleasant history for you to read in all the world as the history of your own lives if you would just sit down and record to yourselves from the beginning till now

[1] John Flavel, *The Mystery of Providence* (Edinburgh: Banner of Truth, 2016), pp. 117-128, 132-135.

what God has been to you and done for you. What significant manifestations and displays of his mercy, faithfulness, and love there have been in all the conditions you have passed through. If your hearts do not melt before you have gone half way through that history, they are hard hearts indeed.

Let them be as intensively full as may be. Do not let your thoughts swim like feathers upon the surface of the waters, but sink like lead to the bottom. 'Great are the works of the LORD, studied by all who delight in them' (Psa. 111:2). Not that I think it feasible to sound the depth of providence by our short line. For, 'Your way was through the sea, your path through the great waters; yet your footprints were unseen' (Psa. 77:19). But it is our duty to dive as far as we can, and to marvel at the depth when we cannot touch the bottom.

There are different things to be distinctly pondered and valued in one single providence before you can judge the amount and worth of it. The timeliness of mercy may give it a very great value. When it shall be timed so exactly, and fall out so seasonably as may make it a thousand-fold more considerable to you than the same mercy would have been at another time. Thus when our wants are allowed to grow to an extremity, and all visible hopes fail, then to have relief given, wonderfully enhances the price of such a mercy (Isa. 41:17-18). And then the particular care and kindness of providence to us is a consideration which exceedingly heightens the mercy in itself and endears it to us. So, when in general calamities upon the world, we are exempted by the favour of providence, covered under its wings, when God shall call to us in evil days, 'Come, my people, enter your chambers' (as it is in Isa. 26:19-20).

The beginning of a providence is of special regard and consideration, and by no means to be neglected by us. There are leading providences, which, however slight and trivial they may seem in themselves, yet justly challenge the first rank among providential favours to us because they usher in a multitude of other mercies, and draw a blessed train of happy consequences after them. Every Christian may furnish himself out of his own stock of experience, if he will but reflect and consider the place where he is, the relationships that he has, and the way by which he was led into them.

The instruments employed by providence for you are of a special consideration, and the finger of God is clearly seen by us when we pursue that meditation. For sometimes great mercies shall be conveyed to us by very improbable means, and more probable ones laid aside. A stranger shall be stirred up to do something for you which your near and natural relations had no power or will to do for you. Jonathan, a mere stranger to David, was closer to him and more friendly and useful to him than his own brothers, who despised and slighted him. Ministers have found more kindness and respect from strangers than their own people who are more obliged to them. 'A prophet is not without honour, except in his hometown and among his relatives and in his own household' (Mark 6:4).

Sometimes God's providence comes by the hands of enemies, as well as strangers. 'The earth came to the help of the woman' (Rev. 12:16). God has bowed the hearts of many wicked men to show great kindness to his people (Acts 27:2). At other times God makes use of instruments for the good to his people, who designed nothing but evil and mischief to them. Thus Joseph's brothers were instrumental in his advancement through that very thing through which they designed his ruin (Gen. 50:20).

The design and scope of providence must not escape our thorough consideration of what the aim of providence is. And truly this, of all others, is the most warming and melting consideration. You have the general account of the aim of all providences: 'And we know that for those who love God all things work together for good' (Rom. 8:28). A thousand friendly hands are at work for Christians to promote and bring about their happiness. O this is enough to sweeten the bitterness of providence to us, that we know it shall turn to our salvation (Phil. 1:19).

The respect and relationship providence bears to our prayers is a significant consideration, and a most useful sweet meditation. Prayer honours providence, and providence honours prayer. Great notice is taken of this in Scripture (Gen. 24:45; Dan. 9:20; Acts 12:12). You have had the very petitions you asked of him. Providences have borne the very signatures of your prayers upon them. O how wonderful are such mercies?

Next, in all your observation of providence have special respect to that word of God which is fulfilled and made good to you thereby. This is a clear truth, that all providences have a relationship to the written word. Thus Solomon in his prayer acknowledges that the promises and providences of God went along step by step with his father David all his days, and that his hand (put there for his providence) had fulfilled whatever his mouth had spoken (1 Kings 8:24). So Joshua, in like manner, acknowledges, that 'not one word has failed of all the good things that the LORD your God promised concerning you' (Josh. 23:14). He had carefully observed the relationship the works of God had to his word. He compared them together, and found an exact harmony. And so may you too, if you will compare them as he did …

Ten Ways in Which God's Providence and God's Word Work Together

1. The word tells you that it is your wisdom and interest to keep close to its rules and the duties it prescribes. It tells you that the way of holiness and obedience is the wisest way— 'this is your wisdom' (Deut. 4:5-6 KJV).

Now let the events of providence speak to show whether this is true or not. Certainly it will appear to be so, whether we consider our present comfort or future happiness, both of which we may see daily exposed by departure from duty and secured by keeping close to it. Let the question be asked of the drunkard, adulterer, or profane swearer, when by sin they have ruined body, soul, estate, and name, whether it be their wisdom to walk in those forbidden paths after their own lusts? Would they not have been better off pursuing their own interest and comfort by keeping within the bounds and limits of God's commands? And they cannot but confess that their way is their folly? 'But what fruit were you getting at that time from the things of which you are now ashamed? For the end of those things is death' (Rom. 6:21). Those who walk in God's statutes escape all of these woes and miseries. Look upon all the ruined estates and bodies you may everywhere see, and behold the truth of the Scriptures evidently made good in those sad providences.

2. The word tells you that your departure from the way of integrity, to make use of sinful policies, shall never profit you (1 Sam. 12:21; Prov. 3:5). Let the events of providence speak to this also. Ask your own experience, and you shall have a full confirmation of this truth. Did you ever leave the way of integrity to bring about your own designs, and prosper in that way? Certainly God has cursed all the ways of sin and, whoever finds they thrive in them, his people shall not. Israel would not rely upon the Lord, but trust in the shadow of Egypt, and what advantage had they by this sinful policy (Isa. 30:1-5)? David used a great deal of sinful policy to cover his wicked fact—but it did not prosper (2 Sam. 12:12)!

3. The word prohibits your trust and confidence in created things, even in the greatest and most powerful among creatures (Psa. 146:3). It tells us that it is better to trust in the Lord than in them (Psa. 18:8). It forbids us putting our confidence in those creatures most nearly allied and related in the bonds of nature to us (Mic. 7:5), and it curses the man

who gives that reliance to the creature which is due to God (Jer. 17:5).

Consult the events of providence in this case, and see whether the word is not confirmed in them. Whatever we have over-loved, idolized and leaned upon, God has from time to time broken, and made us to see the vanity of it. So it is that we find that the best course to be rid of our comforts is to set our hearts inordinately or immoderately upon them! For our God is a jealous God, and will not share his glory with another. If David says, 'my mountain shall stand strong, I shall not be moved', the next news he shall hear is of darkness and trouble (cf. Psa. 30:6-7). How true and faithful do we find these sayings of God to be! Who cannot but agree and say, Your word is truth?

4. The word assures us that sin is the cause and inlet of affliction and sorrow, and that there is an inseparable connection between them. 'Be sure your sin will find you out' (Num. 32:23). That is, the sad effects and afflictions that follow it shall find you out. 'If his sons forsake my law and do not follow my statutes, if they violate my decrees and fail to keep my commands, I will punish their sin with the rod, their iniquity with flogging' (cf. Psa. 89:30-32).

I do not say that God never afflicts his people except for their sin. For he may do it for their trial (1 Pet. 4:12). Nor do I say that God follows every sin with a rod, for who then should stand before him (Psa. 130:3)? But this I say, that it is God's usual way to visit the sins of his people with rods of affliction, and this is in mercy to their souls. And if we would carefully search out the seeds and principles of those miseries under which we or ours do groan, we should find them to lie in our own turnings aside from the Lord (Jer. 2:19; 4:18). Have not all these cautions and threatenings of the word been exactly fulfilled by providence in your own experience? Who can but see the infallible truth of God in all that he has threatened? And no less evident is the truth of the promises to all that will observe how providence makes them good every day to us.

5. How great security God has given to his people in the promises, that no man shall lose anything by self-denial for his sake. Jesus has told us, 'Truly, I say to you, there is no one who has left house or brothers or sisters or mother or father or children or lands, for my sake and for the gospel, who will not receive a hundredfold now in this time, houses and brothers and sisters and mothers and children and lands, with persecutions, and in the age to come eternal life' (Mark. 10:29-30).

Though that vile apostate Julian [the 4th-century Roman Emperor whose reign was marked by hostility towards Christianity] derided this promise, yet thousands and ten thousands have experienced it, and at this day stand ready to set their seal to it. God has made it good to his people, not only in the spiritual realm with inward joy and peace, but in the temporal realm also. Instead of natural relationships, who took care for them before, hundreds of Christians shall stand ready to assist and help them. So, though they have left all for Christ, yet they may say with the Apostle, 'having nothing, yet possessing everything' (2 Cor. 6:10). O the admirable care and tenderness of providence over those who, for conscience sake, have left all, and cast themselves upon its immediate care! Are there not at this day to be found many so provided for, even to the envy of their enemies, and their own wonder? Who cannot see the faithfulness of God in the promises, who has but a heart to trust God in them!

6. The word of promise assures us that whatever wants and difficulties the saints fall into their God will never leave them, nor forsake them (Heb. 13:5), and that he will be with them in trouble (Psa. 91:15).

Consult the various providences of your life to this point, and I do not doubt that you will find the truth of these promises as often confirmed as you have been in trouble. Ask your own hearts, where or when was it that your God forsook you, and left you to sink and perish under your burdens? I do not doubt but most of you have been at one time or other plunged in difficulties out of which you could see no way of escape by the eye of reason, difficulties which staggered your faith in the promise. Ask your own souls the question, and they will satisfy it: did God abandon and cast you off in the day of your difficulties?

7. You read that the word of God is the only support and relief to a gracious soul in the dark day of affliction (Psa. 119:50, 92; 2 Sam. 28:5). It was written for this very purpose (Rom. 15:4). No rules of moral prudence or no sensual remedies can do for us what the word can do. And is not this a certain truth, attested by a thousand undeniable experiences? The saints have found their comforts in God's word when fainting under the rod. One word of God can do more than ten thousand words of men to relieve a distressed soul. The promises of God may

- assure you that the Lord will be with you in trouble (Psa. 91:15); or

- encourage you from inward peace to bear cheerfully outward burdens (John 16:33); or

- satisfy you with God's tenderness and moderation in his dealings with you (Isa. 27:8); or

- satisfy you that you shall reap blessed fruits from them (Rom. 8:28); or

- confirm your security in God and his love under your afflictions (2 Sam. 7:14).

If providence has at any time directed you to one such promise then what real comfort and relief ensue! How light is your burden, compared with what it was before!

8. The word tells us that there is no such way to improve our conditions as to give them out with a cheerful liberality for God, and that our withholding our hands [from those in need] when God and duty call to distribute, will not be for our advantage (see Prov. 11:24-25; 19:17; Isa. 32:8). Consult providence now and you shall find it in all respects according to the report of the word. O how true is the Scripture testimony in it! There are many thousand witnesses now living who can set their seals to both parts of the conviction that what men save (as they count saving) with one hand, providence scatters by another hand. And what they scatter abroad with a liberal hand, and single eye for God, is surely repaid to them, or to theirs. Never did any man lose by distributing for God. He that lends to the poor puts his money to earn interest from the Lord. Some have observed how providence has doubled all they have laid out for God in ways unexpected to them.

9. The word assures us that the best expedient for a man to settle his own place in the consciences and affections of men is to direct his ways so as to please the Lord (Prov. 16:7). And does not providence confirm it? This the three Jews found by experience (Dan. 3:28-29) and so did Daniel (Dan. 6:20-22). This kept up John's reputation in the conscience of Herod (Mark 6:10). So it fell out when Constantine made the decree [legalising Christianity in 313 AD]—those who had kept their faith were in favour and those who changed their religion expelled. Never did any man lose at last by his faithfulness.

10. The written word tells us that the best expedient for inward peace and tranquility of mind under puzzling and distracting troubles is to commit ourselves and our case to the Lord (Psa. 37:5-7; Prov. 16:3). And as you have read in the word, so you have found it in your own experience. O what a burden is off your shoulders when you have resigned the case to God! Then providence orders your affairs comfortably for you. The difficulty is soon over when the heart is brought to this ...

Putting God's Providence to Work in Your Heart

Lastly, work up your hearts to this condition, and exercise those affections which the providences of God around you call for (Eccles. 7:14). Be ready to answer the design and purpose of God in all providences. As there are various affections planted in your souls, so are there several graces planted in those affections, and several providences appointed to draw forth and exercise these graces.

When the providences of God are sad and wounding, either upon the church in general or your families and persons in particular, then it is seasonable for you to exercise godly sorrow and humility of spirit, for in that day and by those providences God calls us to it (Isa. 22:12; Mic. 6:9). Pleasure and natural joy are out of season (Ezek. 21:10). Should we then make mirth? If there is a filial spirit in us we cannot be light and vain, when our Father is angry. And if we possess any real sense of the evil of sin which provokes God's anger, we must be heavy-hearted when God is smiting for it. Also, if we have any awareness of, and compassion for, the miseries that sin brings upon the world, it will make us say with David, 'I look at the faithless with disgust, because they do not keep your commands' (Psa. 119:158). It is sad to consider the miseries that they pull down upon themselves in this world and in the world to come. If there is any concern in us to prevent utter ruin, and stop God in the way of his anger, we know this is the means to do it (Amos 4:12).

However sad and dismal the face of Providence is, yet still maintain spiritual joy and comfort in God under all. Though there are no cattle in the stalls, yet I will rejoice in the Lord, I will be joyful in the God my Saviour (Hab. 3:17). There are two sorts of comforts: one sort is natural and senses-related, and the other sort is divine and spiritual. There is a time when it becomes Christians to exercise both (so Esther 9:22).

And there is a time when the former is to be suspended and laid by (Psa. 137:2). But there is no season wherein spiritual joy and comfort in God is unseasonable (1 Thess. 5:16; Phil. 4:4).

This spiritual joy or comfort is nothing else but the cheerfulness of our heart in God, and the sense of our belonging in him, and in his promises. And it is sure that no providence can render this unseasonable to a Christian. Let us suppose the most afflicted and calamitous state in which a Christian can be involved. Yet, why should sad providences make him lay by his comforts in God, while his afflictions are but for a moment, but divine comforts are eternal (2 Cor. 4:17)? And why should we lay by our joy in God on the account of sad external providences, when at the very worst and lowest ebb, the saints have infinitely more cause to rejoice than to be cast down? There is more in one of their mercies to comfort them than in all their troubles to cast them down. All your losses are but as the loss of a farthing to a prince (Rom. 8:18). *God's heart is full of love, while the face of providence is full of frowns.*

Why should we be cast down under sad providence, when we have so great security, that even by the hand of these providences God will do us good, and all these things shall turn to our salvation? (Rom. 8:28). By these God is but killing your lusts, weaning your hearts from a vain world, preventing temptations, and exciting desires for heaven. This is all the hurt they shall do, and shall that sadden us?

Why should we lay down our joy in God when the change of our condition is so near? It is but a little while, and sorrows shall flee away. Soon you shall not suffer any more: God will wipe away all tears (Rev. 7:17). Well then, you see there is no reason on the account of providence to give up your joy and comfort in God. But if you want to maintain your comfort under all providences, then be careful sure you find your security in God. Faith may be separated from comfort, but assurance cannot.

Mortify your love for earthly things. This makes providences that deprive us and cross us so heavy. Mortify your opinions and loves and you will noticeably lighten your affliction. It is a strong affection that makes strong affliction.

Exercise heavenly-mindedness, and keep your hearts upon things eternal, under all the providences with which the Lord exercises you in this world (Gen. 6:9). Noah walked with God, yet met with as sad providences in his day as any man that ever lived since his time. But alas, we find most providences as *stops* rather than as *steps* in our walk with God. If we are under comfortable providences, how sensual, wanton, and worldly do our hearts grow! And if sad providences befall us, how sluggish or distracted are we! And this comes to pass partly through the narrowness, but mostly through the deceitfulness of our spirits. Our hearts are narrow, and do not know how to manage two businesses of such different natures—as earthly and heavenly matters are—without detriment to one. Others have attained it, and why not we? Prosperous providences are for the most part a dangerous state to the soul.

And certainly, if it were not possible to maintain heavenly-mindedness in such a state and posture of affairs, God would never exercise any of his people with such providences. He would never give you so much of the world to lose your hearts in the love of it or so little to distract you with the cares of it. If therefore we were more deeply sanctified, then the tendencies of our hearts would be more heavenward, ardent and vigorous. If we were more mortified to earthly things, and could but keep our due distance from them, our outward conditions would not at the same rate draw forth and exercise our inward corruptions. Nor would we risk the loss of so sweet an enjoyment as our fellowship with God for the sake of any concerns our bodies have on earth.

In all providences maintain a contented heart with what the Lord allots you, be it more or less of the things of this world. This grace must run parallel with all providences. Learn how to be content whatever the circumstances (Phil. 4:12).

Further Reading

- John Flavel, *The Mystery of Providence* (Edinburgh: Banner of Truth, 2016).

- John Flavel, 'The Fountain of Life', in *The Works of John Flavel*, vol. 1 (Edinburgh: Banner of Truth, 2015).

- *The Works of John Flavel*, 6 vols. (Edinburgh: Banner of Truth, 2015).

- John Flavel, *Keeping the Heart* (Fearn, Ross-shire: Christian Focus, 2012).

THOMAS BOSTON
on the Bible

'A commonplace genius. With the emphasis on genius.' That was the verdict of Thomas Boston (1676–1732) from a minister who lived a century after him. Boston was a man who lived close to God and was dedicated to bringing the love of God in Jesus Christ to all he could. This deeply learned man put that learning to the service of the gospel.

Some might question whether Boston could be defined as a Puritan, given that he exercised his ministry a generation after the close of the Puritan period. But, as a man steeped in Puritan writings and pursuing the same priorities as his seventeenth-century forebears, he deserves attention as a classic example of the Puritan legacy.

Boston was born in Duns in 1676, a small market town ten miles north of the River Tweed, the natural border between Scotland and England. Influenced by his father's godly life, Boston was twelve when he felt the Spirit's power through gospel preaching and was won to Jesus Christ. After graduating from Edinburgh University, he was ordained to the parish of Simprin, close to his home town. Eight years later he was called to Ettrick, a parish in the hills above Selkirk, where he remained until his death in 1732.

Boston's life was not easy. He laboured in a remote part of the Scottish Borders with few opportunities for fellowship with other pastors. He was an acutely sensitive man, and agonized about his own soul, as well as the souls of many others. The trials of ministering to a scattered rural community, many of whom were indifferent to his work, was exhausting and often discouraging. But God used his trials, to shape him, making him a trusted guide for disciples from all walks of life.

Boston sought to visit everyone in his parish twice each year. He steadily built up the congregation in size and spiritual health with a careful routine of Sunday morning expository ministry coupled with Sunday evening catechism classes in his home. He is said to have preached his first sermon in Ettrick to just seven people. Yet by the end of his life he was administering the Lord's Supper to many hundreds of worshippers.

From an early stage in his ministry Boston was putting his sermons as well as other material into books which reached a wider audience than would ever come to his Borders' valley. Boston left an astounding legacy. He was a pioneer in handling the Hebrew text of the Old Testament. He forged a covenantal theology which sought to be faithful to the letter of Scripture while articulating what Boston believed was the shape of God's redemptive purposes. His works run to twelve volumes, covering a huge range of theological and pastoral subjects. The most influential is *Human Nature in its Fourfold State*. On reading it, Jonathan Edwards said that the book showed that 'Mr Boston is a truly great divine'. It was a bestseller in Boston's day and has been read all over the world ever since.

Things to Look Out For

Through years of painstaking study, Boston revolutionized the understanding of the Hebrew of the Old Testament. It is fitting, therefore, that we turn to a work he wrote on the Bible to see how he treasured it, and how he gives practical steps for understanding and responding to it. Our excerpt comes from 'The Scriptures the Book of the Lord, and the Diligent Study and Search Thereof Recommended and Urged'.

Look for the way Boston moves beyond appeals to the mind in order to engage the heart. That is because what drives our behaviour—in this case reading the Bible—is not just what we think, but ultimately what we love. Boston says of the Scriptures, 'There is a transcendent glory in them and whoever discerns it cannot miss to hug and embrace them.' Ask yourself whether this describes how your feel about the Bible. Boston is not just interested in your understanding of God's word, but also in the growth of your love for the God of the word.

❋

The Scriptures: the Book of the Lord[1]

> Seek and read from the book of the LORD:
> Not one of these shall be missing;
> none shall be without her mate.
> For the mouth of the LORD has commanded,
> and his Spirit has gathered them.
>
> *Isaiah 34:16*

Seven Encouragements for Reading God's Word

1. God requires it of us and commands us to do it. 'Search the Scriptures' (John 5:39 KJV). The Jews had once the Scriptures committed to them. But did God design they should only have them in the temple? No, in their houses also. Only laid up in the ark? No, he designed another chest for them—even their hearts (Deut. 6:6-7). Let the authority of God sway you,

---

[1] *The Whole Works of Thomas Boston*, Vol. 1, ed. Samuel McMillan (Aberdeen: George & Robert King, 1848), pp. 67-76.

then, and as you have any regard to it, to study the Scriptures.

2. The very being of the Bible among us is enough to move us to study it because it is that by which we must stand or fall for ever. The proclaiming of the law publicly is sufficient to oblige the subjects and they cannot plead ignorance, though not everyone of them gets their own copy of it, for every one ought to know the rule of his duty. And sinners will be condemned by it if they do not conform to it, whether they knew it or not (John 3:19).

3. It is an exercise very pleasing to God, if it be done in a right manner, namely, in faith. For by it God speaks to us, and we hear and receive his words at his mouth. Obedient ears are his delight.

The Spirit of God commends it. It was the reason why a commendation was given to the Bereans (Acts 17:11), of Apollos (Acts 17:24), and of Timothy (2 Tim. 3:15). And why does the Spirit of God commend others for this? To recommend the Scriptures to us.

There is a particular blessing annexed to this exercise. Blessed is he who reads (Rev. 1:3). And when the children of God in all ages have sucked the sap of God's word, they have had sweet fellowship with God and the influences of the Spirit to quicken, enlighten, bear fruit in, and comfort their souls.

4. Consider how it has been the way of the people of God to be much addicted to and conversant in the Scripture. So is it true that wisdom is justified of her children (Luke 7:35). Take heed you go forth by the footsteps of the flock and you will not find them in the way of slighting, but prizing of the word of God.

You shall find the saints highly prizing the word (Psa. 19 and 119). What large commendations of the word are there! How sweet it was to Jeremiah: 'Your words were found, and I ate them, and your words became to me a joy and the delight of my heart' (Jer. 15:16). Peter, who heard the voice on the mount of transfiguration, yet prefers the Scriptures to voices from heaven (2 Pet. 1:19). Paul speaks highly of it: 'All Scripture is breathed out by God and profitable for teaching, for reproof, for correction, and for training in righteousness' (2 Tim. 3:16). The martyrs highly prized it and ventured their lives for it. One cast away at sea and swimming for his life on a mast, having five pounds which was all his stock in the one hand and a Bible in the other, and being obliged to let go one of them, kept the Bible and let the five pounds go.

You shall find them much addicted to the study of the word. It was David's companion and bosom oracle (Psa. 119:97). Daniel in Babylon searches the Scriptures of the prophets (Dan. 9:2). So did the noble Bereans, Apollos and Timothy.

The Spirit of God makes it the character of a godly man. 'His delight is in the law of the LORD, and on his law he meditates day and night' (Psa. 1:2). O how rational is the man who is born of God who has a natural desire after the word just as the child after the mother's breast (1 Pet. 2:2). The new nature tends to communion with God. It is by the word that the soul has communion with him, for thereby God speaks to us. And therefore it is a sad sign that there are few true Christians while there are so few who diligently ply the word.

5. Consider the excellency of the Scriptures. There is a transcendent glory in them and whoever discerns it cannot miss to hug and embrace them.

It is the best of books. You assume people who have many good books know much, but if you have the Bible then you have the best book in the world. It is the book of the Lord, dictated by unerring infinite wisdom. There is no dross here with the gold; no chaff with the corn. Every word of God is pure. There is nothing for our salvation to be had in other books but what is learned from this. They are but the rivulets that run from this fountain and all shine with light borrowed from the Bible. And it has a blessing annexed to it, a glory and majesty in it, an efficacy with it that no other book has in the same way. Therefore Luther professed he would burn the books he had written rather than allow those books to divert people from reading the Scriptures.

It is the greatest and most excellent of the works of God to be seen in the world (Psa. 138:2). If the world beautified with sun, moon and stars be as a precious ring, the Bible is the diamond in the ring. The sparkling stars and that glorious globe of light the sun yet leave but a dark world where there is no Bible. Were it put to the choice of the saints either to quit the sun out of the firmament or the Bible out of the world, they would chose the former but never the latter. For they cannot want when they can go to the Bible and read all in the face of Jesus. For that must be most excellent that has most of God in it.

It is the oracles of God (Rom. 3:2). This was the chief of the Jewish privileges without which their temple altar and all else would have been but dumb signs. The Pagan world did highly reverence and prize the devil's oracles, but we have God's oracles while we have the Scriptures that manifest to us the secrets of heaven. And if we discern a right who speaks in them we must say it is the voice of God and not of man. Here is what you may consult safely in all your doubts and darknesses; here is what will lead you into all truth.

It is the laws of heaven (Psa. 19:7). The Lord and King of heaven is our great Lawgiver, and the laws are written in this book. It concerns us to study it. We must find our title to heaven, the blessed inheritance, in the Bible, or never obtain it. From hence the sentence of our justification must be drawn, else we are still in a state of wrath. Here is the rule we must follow: that we may please God here. And from this book shall the sentence of our absolution or condemnation be drawn at the great day.

It is Christ's testament and last will (1 Cor. 11:25). Our Lord has died and he has left us this Bible as his testament, and that makes his children have such an affection for it. Here in its pages he has left them his legacy—not only of present blessings, but the eternal inheritance. His last will is now confirmed that shall stand for ever without alteration. So all the believer's hopes are in this Bible and this is the security he has for all the privileges he can lay claim to. This is his charter for heaven, the disposition by which he lays claim to the kingdom. And therefore if you have any interest in the testament, you must not be slighters of it.

It is the sceptre of his kingdom (Psa. 110:2), and it is a sceptre of righteousness. It is by this word that he rules his church and guides all his children in their way to the land that is far off. Wherever he has a kingdom, he wields it. And the nations subjecting themselves to him, receive it. And where he rules in one's heart it has place there too (Col. 3:16). It is a golden sceptre of peace stretched forth to rebels to win them by offering them peace. He offers it to fainting believers to give them peace. And whoever will not subject themselves to it shall be broken with his rod of iron.

It is the channel of influences by which the communications of grace are made and the waters of the sanctuary flow into the soul (Isa. 59).

Lastly, it is the price of blood, even the blood of Christ (1 Cor. 11:25). Had not the personal Word become flesh and died to purchase redemption for us, we would not have seen this written word among us. For it is the book of covenant which is founded on the blood of the Mediator. It is the grant and conveyance of the right to the favour of God, and all saving benefits to believers which they could not have received had not Christ died. And what a slight it will be to tread underfoot the blood of the covenant.

6. Consider the usefulness of the word. If we consider the author we may be sure of the usefulness of work. The Apostle tells us that it alone is sufficient to the man of God, to make

him perfect and thoroughly equip him for all works (2 Tim. 3:16-17). There is no case a soul can be in but it is suitable to their case for those who desire to make use of it. To commend it to you from its usefulness I will make these points:

It is a treasure to the poor and such are we all by nature (Rev. 3:17; 2 Cor. 4:7). Therefore the Lord bids us search the Scriptures like those that search in mines for silver and gold. If the poor soul searches here, receiving the word by faith, he is filled up. He shall find there the discharge of his debt, a new right and title to the mortgaged inheritance. This word of the Lord is a treasure:

A treasure in its worth. People only regard as treasures valuable things. There is nothing in the Scriptures but what is highly valuable. There are the eternal counsels of God touching our salvation, life and immortality, brought to light. There are the purest precepts, the most awful threatenings and the most precious promises (2 Pet. 1:4ff).

A treasure in its variety. In the Scriptures shine the manifold wisdom of God. Some people grow weary of this book of the Lord because, after some time perusing it, they do not feel they find new things in it. But they are not exercising their senses with discernment. For no matter how often we come to the word, if we come bringing fresh affections with us, we find fresh entertainment there. This is evident from the glorious refreshment we sometimes find in a word that we have gone over many times previously without finding anything remarkable in it. And truly, the saints shall never exhaust it while here on earth. Just as new discoveries are made in it at different times, so it will be to the end.

A treasure in its abundance. There is in it, treasure not only for the present but for the time to come (Isa. 42:23). There is abundance of light, instruction, comfort and what is needful for the saints travelling heavenward (Psa. 119:162). And indeed, it is the victory spoil to be gathered by us. Our Lord, having fought the battle against death and devils, here the spoil lies to be gathered by us that remained at home when the fight was on.

A treasure in its closeness. This word contains the wisdom of God in a mystery. It is a hidden book to most of the world and indeed a sealed book to those that remain in their natural blindness. Nor can we get into the treasure without the illumination of the same Spirit which dictated it (1 Cor. 2:10). There is a path here which the vulture's eye has not seen, and which the carnal eye cannot take up (verse 14). Therefore we need to seek diligently and pray: 'Open my eyes, that I may behold wondrous things out of your law' (Psa. 119:18).

It is life to the dead. The words that I speak to you, says Christ, they are spirit and they are life (John 6:63). We are naturally dead in sins, but the word is the means of spiritual life. It is the ordinary means of conversion. The law of the Lord revives the soul (Psa. 19:7). Being born again of incorruptible seed by the word of God (1 Pet. 1:23). By it the soul is persuaded into the covenant and brought to embrace Jesus Christ. For thereby the Spirit is communicated to the elect of God. Thus it is of use to bring sinners home to God from under the power of darkness to the kingdom of his dear Son.

It is light to the blind. 'The commandment of the LORD is pure, enlightening the eyes' (Psa. 19:8). It is a convincing light to enable a person to discover their state before God and so arouse the soul from its natural security. It pierces the heart as an arrow, and makes the careless sinner stand and consider his way, for it freely tells everyone his faults (James 1). And while the child of God travels through the world, it serves to light his way in a dark place, and lets him see how to set step (2 Pet. 1:19). Hence David says, 'Your word is a lamp to my feet and a light to my path' (Psa. 119:105).

It is awakening to those that are asleep (Song of Sol. 7:9). It is the voice of God which is full of majesty to sleepy Christians, calling them to the exercise of grace. For, as it is the means of giving birth to grace in the heart, so it is also the means of actuating and quickening it. Your word preserves my life (Psa. 119:50). Here the Christian may sound the alarm to rise up and be doing. Here are the promises as cords of love to draw us, and the awful threatenings to set idlers to work.

It is a sword of the Christian soldier. 'The sword of the Spirit, which is the word of God' (Eph. 6:17). Whoever has a mind for heaven must fight his way to it. None get the crown except the conquerors (Rev. 3:21). They must go through many temptations, from the devil, world and the flesh, and the word is the sword for resisting of those temptations. It is an offensive and defensive weapon. See how our Lord Jesus wielded it: 'It is written, "Man shall not live by bread alone, but by every word that comes from the mouth of God." Again it is written, "You shall not put the Lord your God to the test"' (Matt. 4:4, 7). If we are well-versed in the word, we may bring answers from it to all our temptations.

It is a counsellor to those who are in straits, doubts and difficulties. Your testimonies are my counsellors (Psa. 119:24). Many a time the children of God, when tossed with doubts and fears, have found a quiet harbour there, have got their way cleared to them there, when they do not know what to do. And no doubt, if we were more exercised to godliness and looking to the Lord in our straits, we would make more use of the Bible as the oracles of heaven.

It is a comforter to those that are cast down. 'Remember your word to your servant, in which you have made me hope. This is my comfort in my affliction, that your promise gives me life' (Psa. 119:49-50). The way to heaven lies through many tribulations, and afflictions are the trodden path to glory. But the Lord has left his people the Bible as a cordial to support them under all their pressures from within and without. And indeed, the sap of the word and the sweetness of the promises are never relished in a more lively way than when the people of God are exercised under afflictions. The heavenly fountain flows at its most plentiful rate when, created streams being dried up, the soul goes for all to the Lord.

Lastly, it is a cure for all diseases of the soul. My words are health to all their flesh. (Prov. 4:22). There is no malady that a soul is under but there is a suitable remedy for it in the word. 2 Timothy 3:16-17, frequently quoted above, is adapted by infinite wisdom to the case of poor sinners. By it the simple may be made wise, the weak strengthened, the staggering confirmed, the hard heart melted, the shut heart opened, it being the means the Spirit uses of for these and all other such purposes.

7. Consider the danger of slighting the word. It exposes sin and consequently the greatest danger. Can they keep the way of the word that do not study to acquaint themselves with it? They must walk in darkness who do not make use of the light, and this leads to everlasting darkness (John 3:19). If by this word we are judged, how can they think to stand that neglect it?

Practical Steps for Reading the Bible

I conclude with some directions for the study of the Scriptures.

1. Keep to an ordinary [a Bible reading plan] that you may become acquainted with the whole and make this reading a part of your secret duties. Not that you should bind yourself to a plan so that you never to read by choice. But this leads most to edification. Some places are difficult and some may seem very bare for an ordinary reader. But if you look on it all as God's word, not to be slighted but read it with faith and reverence, there is no doubt you will find much to your advantage.

2. Set a special mark one way or other on those passages you read which you find most suitable to your case or temptations, or such as you have found to move hearts more than other passages. And it will be wise often to review these.

3. Compare one Scripture with another, the more obscure with that which is more plain (2 Pet. 1:20). This is an excellent way to find out the sense of the Scriptures. To do this, use the marginal notes in your Bible. And keep Christ in your eye, for to him the Scriptures of the Old Testament look (in its genealogies, types and sacrifices), as well as those of the New.

4. Read with a holy attention arising from the consideration of the majesty of God and the reverence due to him. This must be done with attention to the words, to the sense and to the divine authority of the Scripture and the bond it lays on the conscience for obedience (1 Thess. 2:13).

5. Let your main goal in reading the Scriptures be practice and not bare knowledge (James 1:22). Read that you may learn and do, and that without any limitation or distinction, but that whatever you see God requires, you may study to practice.

6. Beg of God and look to him for his Spirit. For it is the Spirit that dictated it, that it must be savingly understood (1 Cor. 2:11). And therefore before you read it is highly reasonable that you beg a blessing on what you are to read.

7. Beware of a worldly, fleshly mind, for fleshly sins blind the mind from the things of God and the worldly heart cannot favour them. In an eclipse of the moon the earth comes between the sun and the moon and so

keeps the light of the sun from it. So the world in the heart, coming between you and the light of the word, keeps its divine light from you.

8. Labour to be exercised towards godliness and to observe your case, for an exercised frame helps mightily to understand the Scriptures. Such a Christian will find his case in the word, and the word will give light to his case and his case light into the word.

9. Lastly, whatever you learn from the word labour to put it in practice. For to him that has, more shall be given. No wonder they get little insight into the Bible who make no conscience of practising what they know. But as long as the stream runs into a holy life, the fountain will be the freer.

Further Reading

- Thomas Boston, *The Crook in the Lot* (Edinburgh: Banner of Truth, 2017).

- Thomas Boston, *Memoirs* (Edinburgh: Banner of Truth, 1988).

- Thomas Boston, *Human Nature in Its Fourfold State* (Edinburgh: Banner of Truth, 2015).

- *The Complete Works of Thomas Boston*, 12 vols. (Stoke-on-Trent: Tentmaker Publications, 2002).

- Andrew Thomson, *Thomas Boston: His Life and Times* (Fearn, Ross-shire: Christian Focus, 2004).

The Banner of Truth Trust publishes a large

number of books by Puritan authors.

Please visit **banneroftruth.org** to browse

our complete catalogue.

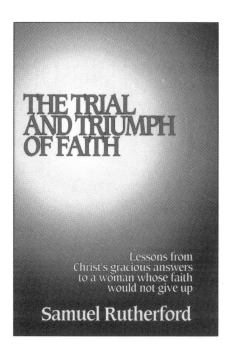

The Trial and Triumph of Faith
Samuel Rutherford

ISBN 978 0 85151 806 0 | 416pp. | paperback

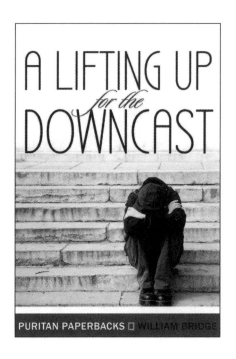

A Lifting Up for the Downcast
William Bridge

ISBN 978 0 85151 298 3 | 288 pp. | paperback

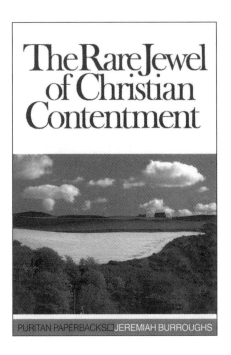

The Rare Jewel of Christian Contentment
Jeremiah Burroughs

ISBN 978 0 85151 091 0 | 232 pp. | paperback

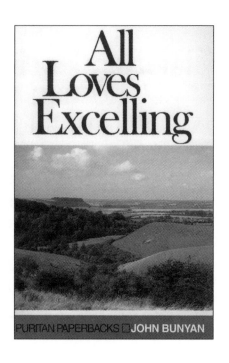

All Loves Excelling

John Bunyan

ISBN 978 0 85151 739 1 │ 139 pp. │ paperback

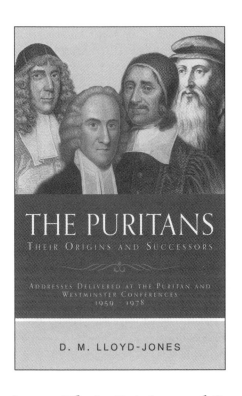

The Puritans: Their Origins and Successors
D. Martyn Lloyd-Jones

ISBN 978 1 84871 470 0 | 440 pp. | clothbound

About the Publisher

The Banner of Truth Trust originated in 1957 in London. The founders believed that much of the best literature of historic Christianity had been allowed to fall into oblivion and that, under God, its recovery could well lead not only to a strengthening of the church, but to true revival.

Interdenominational in vision, this publishing work is now international, and our lists include a number of contemporary authors, together with classics from the past. The translation of these books into many languages is encouraged.

A monthly magazine, *The Banner of Truth,* is also published, and further information about this, and all our other publications, may be found on our website or by contacting either of the offices below.

THE BANNER OF TRUTH TRUST

3 Murrayfield Road
Edinburgh, EH12 6EL
UK

P O Box 621, Carlisle
Pennsylvania 17013
USA

banneroftruth.org